Mastering Live Performance & Touring-Pro Level Tips and Hints to Elevate Your Stage Presence and Tour Like a Pro

Neil J Milliner

Published by Neil J Milliner, 2024.

While every precaution has been taken in the preparation of this book, the publisher assumes no responsibility for errors or omissions, or for damages resulting from the use of the information contained herein.

MASTERING LIVE PERFORMANCE & TOURING-PRO LEVEL TIPS AND HINTS TO ELEVATE YOUR STAGE PRESENCE AND TOUR LIKE A PRO

First edition. October 20, 2024.

ISBN: 979-8227727855

Written by Neil J Milliner.

Also by Neil J Milliner

Artful Investments: Enhancing Your Property Value Through Fine Art
E-commerce SEO Strategies: Selling Online Successfully
Fast Track Your Songwriting Career-Essential Tips and Hints to
Master Your Craft and Build a Lasting Career
The Ultimate Singer's Guide-Practical Tips to Improve Your Voice and
Achieve Your Vocal Dreams
Branding & Networking Success for Bands
Mastering Fan Engagement-Pro-Level Hints to Create Authentic
Connections and Build Loyalty
Mastering Live Performance & Touring-Pro Level Tips and Hints to
Elevate Your Stage Presence and Tour Like a Pro
Music Production Mastery-Step-by-Step Tutorials to Fast-Track Your
Way to Professional Success
The Musician's Tech Toolbox-Essential Technical Tips and Equipment
Know-How for Musicians
The Ultimate Musician's Website Guide-Step-by-Step Tutorials to
Engage Fans and Showcase Your Talent

Contents

Great stage presence is the result of preparation, confidence, and a genuine connection with your music and your audience. By mastering these techniques, you'll not only captivate your listeners but also elevate your overall performance. Keep practicing, stay true to yourself, and remember that each performance is an opportunity to grow as an artist.

Effective Tips to Instantly Improve Your Stage Presence and Engage Your Audience

Effective Tips to Instantly Improve Your Stage Presence and Engage Your Audience

Effective Tips for Talking Onstage Between Songs: How to Engage Your Audience Like a Pro

Effective Tips for Talking Onstage Between Songs: How to Engage Your Audience Like a Pro

Tips for Filling Seats at Your Live Events

Live Show Promotion: Filling Seats and Selling Tickets At Your Live Events

Musician's Health: Addressing Common Performance-Related Issues

Musician's Health: Addressing Common Performance-Related Issues

How to Improve Stage Presence: Essential Performance Tips for Singers to Captivate Audiences

How to Improve Stage Presence: Essential Performance Tips for Singers to Captivate Audiences

FOR SINGERS, DELIVERING a powerful vocal performance is just one piece of the puzzle. Captivating your audience requires great stage presence—a combination of confidence, body language, and connection with the crowd. Whether you're a beginner or a seasoned performer, mastering stage presence can transform your live shows, leaving a lasting impression on your audience.

Here are essential performance tips to help you improve your stage presence and captivate audiences:

1. Project Confidence

CONFIDENCE IS KEY TO strong stage presence. Even if you're nervous, learning how to project confidence can make your performance shine.

- Tip: Practice power poses before going on stage. Standing tall with your shoulders back not only improves your posture but also boosts your confidence. Avoid slouching or timid movements on stage—stand tall, own the space, and engage with your audience through eye contact and smiles.

- Tip: If you feel nervous, channel that energy into your performance. Confidence often comes from preparation, so rehearse regularly and focus on feeling comfortable with your material.

2. Connect With Your Audience

GREAT STAGE PRESENCE is all about building a connection with your audience. The more engaged they feel, the more memorable your performance will be.

- Tip: Make eye contact with different sections of the crowd. Even if you can't see everyone due to stage lighting, look in their general direction to create a sense of intimacy.

- Tip: Talk to your audience between songs. A few genuine words—like sharing the story behind a song or thanking them for coming—can make them feel more connected to you as an artist.

3. Use Dynamic Body Language

YOUR BODY LANGUAGE speaks volumes on stage. Movement can enhance the emotions of your songs and energize your performance, but it needs to be natural and intentional.

- Tip: Avoid standing still for too long. Incorporate gentle swaying, walking across the stage, or hand gestures that match the mood of your music. Use the stage to your advantage, moving from side to side to engage more of your audience.

- Tip: Focus on how your body naturally responds to the music when you sing. Practice in front of a mirror to ensure your movements enhance, rather than distract from, your performance.

4. Master Your Facial Expressions

FACIAL EXPRESSIONS are a subtle yet powerful aspect of stage presence. The way you express emotion while singing can deeply affect how the audience connects with your performance.

- Tip: Match your facial expressions to the lyrics and mood of the song. If you're singing an emotional ballad, let that emotion reflect on your face. For upbeat songs, show excitement and joy through smiles and raised eyebrows.

- Tip: Avoid blank or forced expressions. Practice emoting naturally in rehearsals to make sure your facial expressions come across as genuine.

5. Engage With the Music

STAGE PRESENCE ISN'T just about moving your body; it's about being fully immersed in the music. When the audience sees that you are genuinely engaged with the song, they will be drawn into your performance.

- Tip: Focus on feeling the rhythm, melody, and lyrics. Let the music guide your movements and facial expressions, and don't be afraid to lose yourself in the moment.

- Tip: If you play an instrument while singing, engage with it as part of your stage presence. Use body language and gestures that align with the emotion of your playing.

6. Practice Performing Live

STAGE PRESENCE CAN be improved over time through experience and practice. The more you perform live, the more comfortable and natural you will feel on stage.

- Tip: Rehearse your live performances as if you're on stage. Create a mock stage setup at home and practice performing in front of a mirror or recording yourself. Review the footage to identify areas where you can improve.

- Tip: Start with smaller live shows or open mics to gain confidence and experience. Gradually work your way up to larger venues as you grow more comfortable with performing.

Final Thoughts

IMPROVING YOUR STAGE presence is essential for captivating your audience and delivering unforgettable performances. By projecting confidence, connecting with your audience, using dynamic body language, and engaging with the music, you can transform your live shows. With practice and dedication, you'll feel more comfortable on stage, allowing your authentic self to shine through and leaving a lasting impression on those who watch you perform.

Common Mistakes to Avoid During Live Performances: Essential Tips for Bands and Solo Artists

Performing live is one of the most thrilling aspects of being a musician. It's a chance to connect with your audience and showcase your skills. However, live performances come with their own set of challenges. Whether you're a solo artist or part of a band, certain mistakes can hinder your performance and leave a lasting negative impression on your audience. Here are some common mistakes to avoid during live performances and essential tips to ensure a successful show.

1. Not Being Well-Rehearsed

ONE OF THE MOST OBVIOUS mistakes is going on stage under-rehearsed. Failing to practice enough can lead to forgotten lyrics, missed cues, and an overall shaky performance.

- Tip: Make sure to rehearse your setlist multiple times before the show, focusing on transitions between songs. For bands, ensure that everyone is familiar with the arrangement and timing of each track. A well-rehearsed performance builds confidence and allows you to engage more naturally with your audience.

2. Ignoring Sound Check

SKIPPING OR RUSHING through a sound check can result in technical issues during your performance, from microphone feedback to unbalanced instrument levels.

- Tip: Always allocate enough time for a proper sound check. Work with the sound engineer to balance vocals, instruments, and backing tracks. Test your gear to ensure everything is functioning correctly and listen to how it sounds on stage. A thorough sound check prevents last-minute surprises.

3. Overloading the Set with New Songs

WHILE IT'S EXCITING to debut new music, playing too many unfamiliar tracks can disconnect your audience, especially if they're attending to hear their favorite songs.

- Tip: Strike a balance between new and familiar songs. Include a mix of crowd-pleasers, older hits, and newer material to keep the audience engaged. If you do play new songs, introduce them briefly to create a personal connection with the audience.

4. Poor Stage Presence

STANDING STILL AND not engaging with the audience can make your performance feel flat, no matter how good the music sounds. Stage presence is key to captivating your listeners and creating a memorable experience.

- Tip: Move around, make eye contact, and interact with the crowd. If you're a solo artist, consider how you can fill the stage visually. For bands, make sure each member contributes to the energy of the performance. Confidence on stage makes your performance more exciting and relatable.

5. Lack of Communication with the Audience

NOT SPEAKING TO THE audience between songs can make your performance feel impersonal. On the flip side, talking too much or rambling can break the flow of your set.

- Tip: Prepare a few engaging things to say between songs, whether it's sharing a story behind the song, thanking the crowd, or asking how they're doing. Keep it short, but meaningful. This helps build a connection without dragging down the momentum of the show.

6. Ignoring Technical Issues

TECHNICAL PROBLEMS are bound to happen during live performances, but how you handle them is crucial. Ignoring them or becoming visibly frustrated can distract from your performance.

- Tip: If you encounter a technical issue, stay calm and address it quickly. Have a backup plan, such as extra cables, batteries, or instruments on hand. If needed, engage the audience with a joke or comment to ease the awkwardness. Remember, the show must go on.

7. Unprepared Transitions Between Songs

AWKWARD SILENCES OR long gaps between songs can kill the energy of your set. Transitions should feel seamless and keep the momentum going.

- Tip: Plan your setlist with smooth transitions in mind. Know which songs flow well into each other and practice switching between them during rehearsals. For bands, communicate with each other through subtle signals to avoid any confusion on stage.

8. Playing Too Loud or Too Quiet

VOLUME IS CRITICAL in live performances. Playing too loud can overwhelm the audience and distort your sound, while playing too quiet can make it hard for the crowd to hear you.

- Tip: Rely on the sound engineer to ensure your levels are balanced. As a performer, monitor the stage sound carefully during sound check, and don't hesitate to ask for adjustments if necessary. Achieving the right volume creates a more enjoyable experience for your audience.

9. Not Engaging with the Band Members

FOR BAND PERFORMANCES, not interacting with each other on stage can make the show feel disjointed and impersonal.
   - Tip: Communicate with your bandmates through body language, eye contact, or quick gestures during the performance. This not only helps the flow of the set but also creates a dynamic and cohesive performance that the audience will notice.

10. Not Being Prepared for an Encore

SOMETIMES, THE AUDIENCE will demand an encore, and not being prepared can leave them disappointed.
   - Tip: Always have one or two extra songs in your back pocket, even if they're not part of the planned set. If the crowd asks for more, be ready to give them something exciting to finish off the night on a high note.

Final Thoughts

LIVE PERFORMANCES ARE about more than just playing music — they're about creating an experience for your audience. Avoiding these common mistakes and following these essential tips will help you deliver a polished, engaging, and memorable performance. Whether you're a solo artist or part of a band, preparation, presence, and adaptability are key to ensuring your live shows leave a lasting impression.

Proven Stage Performance Tips for Singers to Boost Stage Presence and Captivate Audiences

Stage presence is a critical skill for singers, helping them connect with their audience and deliver memorable performances. It's not just about singing well—it's about creating an emotional connection, commanding the stage, and keeping the audience engaged. Here are some proven tips to boost your stage presence and captivate any audience.

1. Connect Emotionally with Your Song

THE FIRST STEP IN CAPTIVATING an audience is to connect deeply with the music you're performing. Understand the emotions behind the lyrics and let those feelings come through in your voice and body language. When you genuinely feel the emotion of the song, the audience will feel it too.

- Tip: Before performing, take time to analyze the lyrics and identify moments in the song that resonate with you emotionally. This will allow you to deliver an authentic performance.

2. Master Your Body Language

HOW YOU MOVE ON STAGE is just as important as how you sing. Engaging body language helps convey confidence, enthusiasm, and emotion. Use the space around you—don't stand still unless it adds to the mood of the song. Move naturally with the rhythm, and don't be afraid to make eye contact with the audience.

- Tip: Practice in front of a mirror or record yourself during rehearsals to see how you move. Focus on keeping your movements fluid and expressive, rather than stiff or forced.

3. Command the Stage with Confidence

EVEN IF YOU FEEL NERVOUS, project confidence. Audiences are drawn to performers who look and act like they belong on stage. Stand tall, take ownership of the space, and use gestures that match the energy of the performance. The more comfortable and confident you appear, the more the audience will respond positively.

- Tip: Try power poses before going on stage to help boost your confidence. Breathing exercises can also help you calm nerves and center yourself before performing.

4. Engage with Your Audience

Interaction with the audience is key to building a connection and keeping them engaged. Make eye contact, acknowledge people in the crowd, and if appropriate, encourage them to sing or clap along. Engaging with the audience creates a shared experience and makes them feel like they are a part of the performance.

- Tip: Take advantage of moments between songs to talk to the crowd. Introduce the next song with a brief story or joke to establish a more personal connection.

5. Work on Your Vocal Dynamics

USING VOCAL DYNAMICS (variations in volume, tone, and intensity) can make your performance much more captivating. Avoid singing at the same volume and intensity throughout the entire song. Create contrast by incorporating soft, intimate moments and building up to powerful, energetic ones.

- Tip: Plan where to use dynamics in your performance to emphasize key moments in the song. This will help keep the audience on the edge of their seats, waiting for the next surprise.

6. Practice Stage Movement

REHEARSING HOW YOU'LL move on stage is crucial. Plan how you'll interact with the microphone stand, whether you'll move across the stage, or how you'll approach key moments like hitting high notes. Strategic movements can elevate your performance and make it visually interesting.

- Tip: Rehearse with the same setup you'll use on stage. This will give you a chance to get used to your surroundings, ensuring you won't be thrown off by the physical aspects of the stage.

7. Stay in the Moment

ONE OF THE MOST IMPORTANT parts of having great stage presence is staying in the moment and reacting to what's happening around you. Whether it's a technical difficulty or a particularly enthusiastic audience member, acknowledging what's going on shows your authenticity and adaptability as a performer.

- Tip: Don't worry about perfection—embrace the unpredictability of live performances. If something unexpected happens, go with it, and use it to your advantage.

8. Control Your Nerves

STAGE FRIGHT IS COMMON, even for seasoned performers. The key is learning to channel that nervous energy into excitement. By focusing on the audience's positive energy and remembering that they're there to support you, you can ease your nerves and focus on delivering a great performance.

- Tip: Before stepping on stage, take slow, deep breaths to calm your nerves. Visualizing a successful performance can also help shift your mindset from anxiety to excitement.

9. Know Your Set Inside and Out

THE MORE COMFORTABLE you are with your songs, the more confident you'll feel on stage. Knowing your material inside and out gives you the freedom to focus on your performance rather than worrying about forgetting lyrics or missing cues. This level of preparation allows for spontaneity and interaction with the audience.

- Tip: Practice performing your set in different environments to simulate various conditions, such as a smaller or larger stage. This will help you adapt more easily to any live setting.

10. Leave a Lasting Impression

MAKE SURE YOU END YOUR performance with impact. Whether it's by hitting a powerful final note, executing a dramatic stage exit, or delivering a heartfelt message to the audience, leave them wanting more. A strong ending can ensure your performance stays in the audience's mind long after the show is over.

- Tip: Plan a memorable closing song and finish with an upbeat or emotional high point to leave your audience with a lasting impression.

Conclusion

Great stage presence is the result of preparation, confidence, and a genuine connection with your music and your audience. By mastering these techniques, you'll not only captivate your listeners but also elevate your overall performance. Keep practicing, stay true to yourself, and remember that each performance is an opportunity to grow as an artist.

Effective Tips to Instantly Improve Your Stage Presence and Engage Your Audience

STAGE PRESENCE IS THE magic that transforms a good performance into an unforgettable experience. Whether you're playing to a packed venue or a small crowd, captivating your audience is essential for any performer. While musical skills are crucial, how you carry yourself on stage plays an equally important role in making a lasting impact. Here are some effective tips to instantly improve your stage presence and keep your audience engaged throughout your performance.

1. Confidence is Key

CONFIDENCE RADIATES from the moment you step on stage. Even if you're nervous, projecting confidence will help you connect with your audience. Remember, most people in the crowd are there to support you, not to judge. They want to enjoy the performance just as much as you do.

- Tip: Practice your set until it feels second nature. The more prepared you are, the more confident you'll feel on stage. Before stepping onto the stage, take a few deep breaths and remind yourself that you're capable of delivering an amazing performance.

2. Make Eye Contact

EYE CONTACT IS ONE of the most powerful tools for engaging with your audience. It creates a personal connection, making people feel like you're performing directly to them.

- Tip: As you perform, make an effort to look at different sections of the audience, rather than focusing solely on one spot. Engage with individuals in the crowd, especially those in the front rows, but don't stare too long—keep it natural and fluid.

3. Move With Purpose

STANDING STIFFLY OR staying in one spot can make your performance feel static, no matter how great the music is. Moving with purpose adds energy and dynamic flair to your performance. It also reflects your emotional connection with the music, which draws in your audience.

- Tip: Practice moving around while you rehearse. Whether it's walking across the stage, stepping forward during key moments, or using hand gestures, your movement should match the tone and mood of the music.

4. Engage with the Crowd

YOUR AUDIENCE ISN'T just there to watch; they want to feel like they're part of the performance. One of the best ways to engage the crowd is by talking to them between songs. Simple interactions like asking how they're doing, sharing a personal story, or getting them to clap or sing along can break the barrier between performer and audience.

- Tip: Learn to read the room. If the crowd seems shy, gently encourage them to participate. If they're already excited, feed off their energy by giving them moments to interact, like inviting them to sing along during the chorus.

5. Express Emotion Through Body Language

YOUR BODY LANGUAGE says as much as your words and music. Expressing emotion through your body, facial expressions, and gestures adds depth to your performance. It allows the audience to feel the music on a deeper level.

- Tip: During rehearsals, explore different ways of using your body to convey the emotions of the song. Let yourself feel the intensity of the music and translate that into your movements—whether it's leaning into a passionate note or stepping back during softer moments.

6. Use Microphone Techniques Effectively

HOW YOU HOLD AND USE the microphone can significantly impact your performance. Proper microphone technique not only ensures that your voice is heard clearly but also adds to the visual aspect of your stage presence.

- Tip: Hold the microphone at the right distance (usually a few inches away from your mouth) for clear sound. For emphasis, you can move closer for softer, intimate parts of the song, or step back for powerful moments to prevent distortion.

7. Connect Emotionally with Your Music

A PERFORMANCE BECOMES truly captivating when the audience can sense that the artist is emotionally invested in their music. Connecting deeply with your songs allows you to convey genuine emotion, which resonates with listeners and keeps them engaged.

- Tip: Think about the story or meaning behind each song and let those emotions guide your performance. Whether it's joy, sadness, anger, or excitement, channel those feelings into how you deliver the song.

8. Dress the Part

HOW YOU PRESENT YOURSELF visually can enhance your stage presence. Your stage outfit should reflect the mood and style of your music while making you feel comfortable and confident.

- Tip: Choose attire that matches the vibe you want to project. If your music is laid-back and acoustic, something more casual might work. For more energetic or intense performances, bolder clothing choices can help create a visual impact.

9. Learn from the Pros

ONE OF THE BEST WAYS to improve your stage presence is by studying other performers who captivate audiences. Whether it's watching live concerts or video performances of your favorite artists, observe how they engage the crowd, move, and interact on stage.

- Tip: Take notes on what stands out to you. What kind of movements do they use? How do they handle mistakes? How do they talk to the audience? Try incorporating elements of what you admire into your own performance style.

10. Adapt and Be Present

NO TWO PERFORMANCES are ever the same. Some audiences may be more enthusiastic, while others might be more reserved. The key is to remain adaptable and present. If something goes wrong—like a technical issue—handle it with grace, humor, and professionalism. Being present and reacting authentically to the moment will show your audience that you're human, and they'll appreciate your honesty.

- Tip: If something unexpected happens, like a broken string or mic failure, don't panic. Acknowledge the situation light-heartedly and keep the energy up. The audience often enjoys seeing how performers handle these moments with composure.

Conclusion

STAGE PRESENCE IS ABOUT more than just performing songs; it's about creating an unforgettable experience for your audience. By building confidence, engaging with the crowd, expressing emotion, and staying present, you can elevate your stage presence to captivate any audience. Remember, stage presence improves with time and practice, so continue honing your skills with each performance, and watch as your connection with listeners grows stronger and more impactful.

Effective Tips for Talking Onstage Between Songs: How to Engage Your Audience Like a Pro

Talking onstage between songs can feel intimidating, but it's one of the best ways to connect with your audience and create a memorable live experience. Mastering the art of speaking between songs can elevate your performance, helping you engage your listeners, share your story, and build a deeper relationship with your fans. Here are some effective tips to help you engage your audience like a pro when talking onstage.

1. Plan, But Don't Script

WHILE IT'S IMPORTANT to have an idea of what you want to say between songs, over-rehearsing or scripting every word can make your interactions feel unnatural. Audiences respond best to authenticity, so allow yourself some flexibility to be in the moment.

How to Prepare:

- Outline talking points: Instead of writing a full script, jot down key points you want to mention, like introducing a new song, telling a personal story, or thanking the audience.

- Practice transitions: Smooth transitions between songs and dialogue will make your performance flow better. Practice moving from one song to the next, ensuring the change feels natural.

- Be adaptable: If the crowd is responding to something you say or do, feel free to deviate from your plan and engage with them directly.

2. Keep It Brief and Engaging

WHEN YOU TALK BETWEEN songs, aim to keep your audience's attention. Long, drawn-out speeches can lose their focus, while short, engaging remarks will keep the energy high.

Tips for Keeping It Engaging:

- Tell a story: Share a quick story about the song you're about to play or an interesting experience you had that day. Audiences love hearing behind-the-scenes moments.

- Ask questions: Engage the crowd by asking simple questions, like "How's everyone feeling tonight?" or "Who's ready to hear this next track?"

- Be relatable: Share personal anecdotes or emotions that your audience can connect with. For example, explain how a song was inspired by a real-life event or feeling.

3. Know Your Audience

TAILORING YOUR ONSTAGE banter to fit your audience is key to building rapport. Different crowds respond to different approaches, so read the room and adjust your tone and content accordingly.

How to Read the Room:

- Consider the venue: A smaller, intimate setting may invite more personal interaction, while a large festival crowd may respond better to high-energy shoutouts and humor.

- Age and vibe of the audience: Pay attention to the demographic of your crowd. Younger audiences may enjoy more casual, humorous banter, while older crowds might appreciate storytelling or thoughtful insights.

- Incorporate local references: If you're playing in a specific city, mention something relevant to the area, whether it's a landmark, a local food you tried, or a past performance in that town.

4. Be Yourself

AUDIENCES CAN TELL when you're being authentic. Rather than trying to adopt a stage persona or mimic another artist's style, focus on speaking in a way that feels natural to you. Whether you're introverted, funny, emotional, or laid-back, let your personality shine through.

How to Stay Authentic:

- Use your natural voice: Don't force yourself to be overly energetic or performative if that's not your style. Speak in a way that feels comfortable and true to yourself.

- Show vulnerability: Don't be afraid to express genuine emotions or talk about challenges you've faced as a musician. Authenticity creates deeper connections with your audience.

- Relax and have fun: Enjoy your time onstage, and your audience will enjoy it with you. Let loose, make jokes, and embrace any awkward moments that come your way.

5. Incorporate Humor and Playfulness

HUMOR IS A POWERFUL tool for breaking the ice and making your audience feel more connected to you. Lighthearted banter between songs can ease the tension, create laughs, and make your performance feel more relaxed and fun.

How to Add Humor:

- Self-deprecating jokes: Don't be afraid to poke fun at yourself or your band. For example, if you forget a lyric, make a joke out of it. Audiences love when musicians show they're human too.

- React to the moment: Use spontaneous moments during your performance—like crowd reactions or technical issues—as an opportunity to inject humor and make the audience laugh.

- Engage with the audience playfully: Make lighthearted comments about audience members' signs, dancing, or even shoutouts from the crowd.

6. Encourage Audience Participation

ENGAGING THE AUDIENCE by inviting them to participate can create an electric atmosphere and elevate the energy in the room. Crowd interaction helps break down barriers and makes your performance more inclusive.

Ways to Get the Audience Involved:

- Call-and-response: Lead the crowd in a call-and-response chant or singing along to a well-known chorus. This makes the audience feel like part of the performance.

- Singalongs: If you're performing a popular or well-known song, encourage the crowd to sing with you. It can be a powerful, unifying moment.

- Clap-along or dance-along: Ask the audience to clap in rhythm during a certain part of a song or get them to dance or sway together. It's a fun way to involve the crowd and heighten the energy.

7. Acknowledge Your Band and Team

A GREAT WAY TO BREAK up your onstage talk is by acknowledging the people who help make the show happen, like your band members, crew, or support act. It adds a level of professionalism and shows your gratitude.

Ways to Give Shoutouts:

- Introduce your band: Between songs, take a moment to introduce your bandmates. It can be as simple as shouting out their names or giving them a moment to shine with a solo.

- Thank the crew: Mention your sound engineers, lighting techs, or tour manager to show appreciation for the behind-the-scenes team.

- Thank the audience: Always thank the crowd for being there, especially if you're playing in a new city or at a special event. A heartfelt thank you goes a long way.

8. Wrap Up with a Memorable Closing

YOUR FINAL WORDS BETWEEN songs (or at the end of your set) should leave a lasting impression. Whether it's a heartfelt message, a call to action, or a reminder about merch or upcoming shows, make sure you close with something impactful.

Effective Ways to End:

- Express gratitude: Thank your audience for their support and presence. End with a positive note that leaves them feeling good.

- Remind them of next steps: Whether it's an invite to the merch table, promoting your next gig, or encouraging fans to follow you on social media, use your last few moments to give a clear call to action.

- End on an emotional high: Whether it's a joke, a heartfelt message, or an inspiring line, leave the audience with something that resonates.

Final Thoughts

TALKING ONSTAGE BETWEEN songs is an art that can take your live performance to the next level. By keeping your dialogue authentic, engaging, and interactive, you can create a deeper connection with your audience and make every performance memorable. Whether you're sharing personal stories, cracking jokes, or getting the crowd involved, the key is to be yourself and enjoy the moment. With these tips, you'll be engaging your audience like a pro in no time!

Tips for Filling Seats at Your Live Events

Promoting a live show is an art in itself. Whether you're an emerging artist or a seasoned performer, filling seats and selling tickets requires a well-thought-out strategy. In today's competitive music scene, simply announcing your gig isn't enough—you need to actively engage with your audience and create a buzz that makes people want to attend. This blog post will guide you through effective techniques to promote your gigs and ensure that you are filling seats at your live events and your live shows are packed.

Understand Your Audience

THE FIRST STEP IN PROMOTING your live show is understanding your target audience. Knowing who they are, what they like, and where they spend their time is crucial to crafting a promotion strategy that resonates.

1. Identify Your Core Fans:

Your core fans are the people most likely to attend your shows. These might be your social media followers, people who have attended your previous gigs, or listeners who regularly stream your music. Understanding their demographics—age, location, interests—helps you tailor your promotional efforts.

2. Segment Your Audience:

Not all fans are the same. Some may prefer intimate acoustic sets, while others might be drawn to high-energy performances. Segment your audience based on their preferences, and target your promotions accordingly.

Utilize Social Media

SOCIAL MEDIA IS ONE of the most powerful tools for promoting live shows. It allows you to reach a broad audience, create excitement, and engage with fans in real time.

1. Create a Social Media Plan:

Develop a content calendar that outlines what you'll post in the weeks leading up to your show. Include announcements, behind-the-scenes content, teasers, and reminders. Use a mix of posts—videos, images, stories, and live streams—to keep your audience engaged.

2. Leverage Multiple Platforms:

Different social media platforms cater to different audiences. Use Instagram and TikTok for visually appealing content, Facebook for event pages and ads, and Twitter for real-time updates. Tailor your content to fit the platform's strengths.

3. Engage with Your Followers:

Don't just post and forget. Engage with your followers by responding to comments, answering questions, and encouraging them to share your content. The more interaction you have, the more likely your posts will reach a wider audience.

4. Use Paid Advertising:

Consider investing in paid social media ads to reach a larger audience. Platforms like Facebook and Instagram allow you to target specific demographics, interests, and locations, making your ads more effective.

Collaborate with Influencers and Local Media

COLLABORATING WITH influencers and local media can significantly boost your show's visibility.

1. Partner with Influencers:

Identify local influencers or bloggers who resonate with your music style and have a following that matches your target audience. They can promote your show through their platforms, offering authentic endorsements that can drive ticket sales.

2. Reach Out to Local Media:

Contact local radio stations, newspapers, and music blogs to feature your upcoming show. An interview, a feature story, or even a simple event listing can help get the word out to potential attendees.

3. Offer Press Passes:

Invite journalists, bloggers, and influencers to attend your show for free in exchange for coverage. This not only increases your show's visibility but also provides you with content that can be used to promote future events.

Create Compelling Promotional Content

THE CONTENT YOU CREATE to promote your live show should capture the essence of your performance and entice people to attend.

1. Design Eye-Catching Posters:

A well-designed poster can grab attention and convey the vibe of your show. Include essential details like the date, time, venue, and ticket information, and make sure the design aligns with your brand.

2. Share Teasers and Trailers:

Create short video teasers or trailers that give a sneak peek of what attendees can expect. Whether it's a snippet of a rehearsal, behind-the-scenes footage, or highlights from past shows, these teasers can build anticipation.

3. Highlight Special Features:

If your show has unique elements—like special guests, a new setlist, or a themed performance—make sure to highlight these in your promotional materials. Give potential attendees a reason to feel they can't miss this particular event.

4. Utilize Email Marketing:

Don't underestimate the power of email marketing. Send out newsletters to your mailing list with all the details of your upcoming show, including links to buy tickets. Personalize the emails to make your fans feel special and valued.

Engage with Your Local Community

Connecting with your local community can be a great way to fill seats for your live show.

1. Partner with Local Businesses:

Team up with local businesses to cross-promote your show. For example, you could offer ticket discounts to customers of a nearby café or give away tickets through a local boutique. These partnerships can help you tap into new audiences.

2. Perform at Local Events:

If possible, perform at local events or festivals in the weeks leading up to your show. This can help you gain exposure and promote your gig to a wider audience.

3. Hand Out Flyers:

Old-school promotion still has its place. Hand out flyers at local hotspots, music stores, and events. Make sure your flyers are visually appealing and include all the necessary details.

Incentivize Ticket Sales

CREATING INCENTIVES can motivate people to purchase tickets in advance.

1. Early Bird Discounts:

Offer discounted tickets to those who buy early. This not only encourages early sales but also helps you gauge interest and plan accordingly.

2. Group Discounts:

Offer discounts for group purchases to encourage people to bring friends. This can be particularly effective for shows in larger venues.

3. Exclusive Perks:

Provide exclusive perks for advance ticket holders, such as early entry, meet-and-greet opportunities, or merchandise discounts. These added incentives can make your show more appealing.

4. Run Contests and Giveaways:

Hold contests on social media where fans can win free tickets or backstage passes. This not only drives engagement but also spreads the word about your show.

Conclusion

PROMOTING A LIVE SHOW requires creativity, strategy, and a deep understanding of your audience. By utilizing social media, collaborating with influencers, creating compelling content, engaging with your local community, and offering incentives, you can effectively promote your gigs and ensure that your shows are well-attended. Remember, the key to successful promotion is consistent effort and genuine connection with your audience. With the right approach, you can turn your live performances into must-attend events that fans eagerly anticipate.

Musician's Health: Addressing Common Performance-Related Issues

Being a musician is not just about talent and creativity; it also demands physical and mental endurance. From long hours of practice to the pressures of live performances, musicians face unique challenges that can take a toll on their health. Ignoring these issues can lead to serious problems that may affect your ability to perform and enjoy your craft. In this blog post, we'll explore common performance-related health issues that musicians face and discuss strategies for prioritizing self-care. Whether you're a seasoned professional or just starting out, taking care of your health is essential for a long and fulfilling career in music.

Understanding the Physical Demands of Musicianship

REPETITIVE STRAIN INJURIES (RSIs)

Repetitive strain injuries are a common issue for musicians, particularly those who play instruments that require repetitive motions, such as guitar, piano, or violin. RSIs can lead to pain, stiffness, and reduced mobility in the affected areas, often in the hands, wrists, and shoulders. To prevent RSIs, it's important to practice good posture, take regular breaks, and incorporate stretching exercises into your routine.

Vocal Strain and Fatigue

For singers, vocal strain is a significant concern. Overuse of the vocal cords, improper technique, and inadequate warm-up can lead to hoarseness, loss of range, and even vocal cord damage. Vocalists should prioritize vocal health by practicing proper technique, staying hydrated, and giving their voice time to rest between performances.

Hearing Loss

Exposure to loud music over extended periods can result in hearing loss, a risk that many musicians face. Protecting your hearing is crucial for maintaining your ability to perform. Consider using earplugs during rehearsals and performances, and try to limit exposure to loud environments outside of work.

Mental Health Challenges in the Music Industry

PERFORMANCE ANXIETY

Performance anxiety, or stage fright, is a common issue for many musicians, regardless of experience level. The pressure to deliver a flawless performance can lead to stress, anxiety, and even panic attacks. Managing performance anxiety requires a combination of preparation, relaxation techniques, and sometimes professional support.

Burnout and Fatigue

The demands of a musician's lifestyle—constant travel, irregular hours, and the pressure to succeed—can lead to burnout and fatigue. Musicians often feel the need to push through these feelings, but doing so can have serious long-term consequences. Recognizing the signs of burnout and taking time to rest and recharge is vital for maintaining mental and physical health.

Depression and Isolation

The music industry can be isolating, especially for solo artists or those who spend a lot of time on the road. The lack of a stable routine, coupled with the pressures of the industry, can contribute to feelings of depression and loneliness. It's important for musicians to build a support network and seek help when needed.

Prioritizing Self-Care as a Musician

DEVELOPING A ROUTINE

Establishing a daily routine that includes time for rest, exercise, and nutrition can help musicians maintain their physical and mental health. A balanced routine allows for recovery and ensures that you're physically prepared for the demands of your craft.

Incorporating Exercise and Physical Therapy

Regular exercise is essential for musicians, particularly those who play physically demanding instruments. Strength training, stretching, and cardiovascular exercise can help prevent injuries and improve overall performance. For those dealing with chronic pain or injuries, working with a physical therapist can provide targeted relief and help you return to playing with confidence.

Mindfulness and Relaxation Techniques

Mindfulness practices, such as meditation and deep breathing exercises, can help musicians manage stress and improve focus. These techniques are particularly useful for dealing with performance anxiety and maintaining mental clarity during performances.

Vocal Health Tips for Singers

Singers should pay special attention to vocal health, as the voice is a delicate instrument. Regular vocal warm-ups, proper technique, and staying hydrated are essential for maintaining vocal strength and preventing strain. Additionally, vocalists should avoid smoking and limit alcohol consumption, as these can have a negative impact on the voice.

Creating a Support System

CONNECTING WITH OTHER Musicians

Building relationships with other musicians can provide emotional support and valuable insights into managing the challenges of a music career. Whether through online forums, local music communities, or industry events, connecting with peers can help you feel less isolated and more supported.

Seeking Professional Help

Don't hesitate to seek professional help if you're struggling with mental or physical health issues. Whether it's working with a therapist, a vocal coach, or a physical therapist, professional support can make a significant difference in your overall well-being.

Balancing Work and Life

Maintaining a healthy work-life balance is crucial for long-term success as a musician. Set boundaries to protect your personal time, and make sure to prioritize activities that bring you joy and relaxation outside of music.

Conclusion

PRIORITIZING SELF-CARE is not just beneficial—it's essential for musicians who want to sustain a long and healthy career. By addressing common performance-related health issues, developing a balanced routine, and seeking support when needed, you can protect your physical and mental well-being while continuing to pursue your passion for music. Remember, your health is your greatest asset, and taking care of it will allow you to enjoy a fulfilling and successful career in the music industry.

FAQs

FAQ 1: WHAT ARE THE most common physical health issues musicians face?

Common physical health issues for musicians include repetitive strain injuries, vocal strain, hearing loss, and fatigue. These issues can be mitigated through proper technique, regular breaks, and self-care practices.

FAQ 2: How can musicians prevent burnout?

Musicians can prevent burnout by establishing a balanced routine that includes time for rest, exercise, and activities outside of music. It's also important to recognize the signs of burnout early and take time to recharge when needed.

FAQ 3: What are some tips for managing performance anxiety?

Managing performance anxiety involves preparation, practicing relaxation techniques like deep breathing, and seeking support from peers or professionals if needed. Building confidence through regular practice and positive self-talk can also help reduce anxiety.

FAQ 4: How can singers protect their vocal health?

Singers can protect their vocal health by practicing proper technique, staying hydrated, avoiding smoking, and giving their voice adequate rest. Regular vocal warm-ups and exercises are also crucial for maintaining vocal strength.

FAQ 5: Why is a support system important for musicians?

A support system provides emotional and professional support, helping musicians navigate the challenges of the industry. Connecting with other musicians, seeking professional help, and maintaining a work-life balance are all important aspects of a strong support system.

Tour Planning: Overcoming Logistics and Scheduling Hurdles

Planning a tour is an exciting yet daunting task. Whether you're a musician hitting the road for the first time or a seasoned band looking to optimize your touring strategy, overcoming logistics and scheduling hurdles is crucial to ensure a successful and stress-free experience. From coordinating travel and accommodations to managing tight schedules, there are many moving parts to consider. In this blog post, we'll explore practical tips and strategies to help you efficiently plan your tour, overcome common challenges, and keep everything running smoothly.

The Importance of Efficient Tour Planning

MAXIMIZING YOUR REACH

One of the primary goals of touring is to reach as many fans as possible. Efficient tour planning allows you to maximize your reach by carefully selecting cities and venues that align with your fanbase. By optimizing your route and schedule, you can perform in more locations without overextending yourself or your team.

Minimizing Costs

Touring can be expensive, with costs for transportation, lodging, meals, and more quickly adding up. Effective planning helps you minimize these costs by identifying the most cost-effective options for travel, accommodation, and other expenses. This allows you to make the most of your budget while still delivering an exceptional experience for your fans.

Ensuring Smooth Operations

A well-planned tour ensures that everything runs smoothly, from load-ins to soundchecks to performances. By addressing logistical challenges ahead of time, you reduce the risk of delays, miscommunications, and other issues that could disrupt your tour. This helps you stay focused on what really matters: delivering great performances and connecting with your audience.

Common Logistics and Scheduling Hurdles

VENUE AVAILABILITY

One of the most significant challenges in tour planning is securing venues that align with your schedule. Popular venues often book up months in advance, making it difficult to find available dates that fit your tour plan.

Travel Coordination

Coordinating travel between cities can be a logistical nightmare. You need to consider the distance between locations, travel time, and the most efficient modes of transportation. Additionally, unexpected issues like traffic, weather, or vehicle breakdowns can throw a wrench in your plans.

Accommodation Challenges

Finding suitable accommodations for your team can be tricky, especially when working with a tight budget. You need to ensure that your team has a comfortable place to rest and recharge after each performance, without breaking the bank.

Scheduling Conflicts

Scheduling conflicts can arise at any time, whether it's a double booking, an unplanned event, or a member of your team having a prior commitment. These conflicts can disrupt your tour and require last-minute adjustments.

Health and Well-being of the Team

Touring can be physically and mentally exhausting. Long hours on the road, irregular sleep schedules, and the demands of performing can take a toll on your team's health and well-being. It's important to plan for rest days and consider the well-being of everyone involved.

Steps to Overcome Tour Planning Hurdles

STEP 1: START PLANNING Early

The earlier you start planning your tour, the better. This gives you more time to secure venues, coordinate travel, and address any potential issues before they become critical. Ideally, start planning at least six months before your intended tour dates.

Step 2: Optimize Your Route

When planning your tour route, consider the geography of your locations to minimize travel time and costs. Group nearby cities together and plan your route in a logical, efficient manner. This not only reduces travel expenses but also minimizes wear and tear on your team.

Step 3: Work with a Reliable Booking Agent

A reliable booking agent can be invaluable in securing venues and managing the logistics of your tour. They have industry connections and experience that can help you navigate the complexities of tour planning. If you don't already have a booking agent, consider hiring one to assist with your tour.

Step 4: Budget Wisely

Create a detailed budget that accounts for all potential expenses, including travel, accommodations, food, equipment, and contingencies. Stick to your budget as closely as possible to avoid financial strain. Look for ways to save money, such as booking group accommodations or using loyalty programs for travel.

Step 5: Use Tour Planning Software

There are several tour planning software options available that can help streamline the logistics of your tour. These tools allow you to manage your schedule, track expenses, and coordinate with your team all in one place. Some popular options include Master Tour and Eventric's LiveTour.

Step 6: Have Backup Plans

Always have backup plans in place for key aspects of your tour, such as alternative routes, backup accommodations, and contingency funds. This ensures that you're prepared for unexpected challenges, such as a venue canceling at the last minute or a vehicle breakdown.

Step 7: Prioritize Communication

Clear and consistent communication with your team, venues, and other stakeholders is essential for a successful tour. Use communication tools like group chats, project management apps, and regular meetings to keep everyone on the same page.

Step 8: Plan for Health and Wellness

Schedule rest days throughout your tour to give your team time to recuperate. Encourage healthy eating, regular exercise, and adequate sleep to maintain everyone's well-being. Consider the mental health of your team as well, and provide support when needed.

Benefits of Efficient Tour Planning

REDUCED STRESS

Efficient tour planning reduces stress for everyone involved. By having a clear plan and addressing potential challenges ahead of time, you can focus on delivering great performances rather than worrying about logistics.

Better Audience Engagement

When your tour is well-organized, you can focus more on engaging with your audience and delivering memorable performances. This leads to a better experience for your fans and can help you build a stronger connection with your audience.

Increased Profitability

By minimizing costs and maximizing efficiency, you can increase the profitability of your tour. This allows you to reinvest in your music, grow your brand, and plan even more successful tours in the future.

Enhanced Team Morale

A well-planned tour keeps your team motivated and energized. When everyone knows what to expect and feels supported, morale stays high, leading to better performances and a more positive experience overall.

Conclusion

TOUR PLANNING IS A complex process that requires careful consideration of logistics, scheduling, and the well-being of your team. By starting early, optimizing your route, working with a reliable booking agent, and using the right tools, you can overcome common hurdles and ensure a successful tour. Remember to prioritize communication, plan for contingencies, and focus on the health and wellness of your team. With the right approach, you can efficiently plan your tour, deliver unforgettable performances, and connect with fans across the globe.

FAQs

FAQ 1: HOW EARLY SHOULD I start planning my tour?

Ideally, you should start planning your tour at least six months in advance. This gives you enough time to secure venues, coordinate travel, and address any potential issues.

FAQ 2: What are some tips for minimizing tour costs?

To minimize tour costs, optimize your route to reduce travel expenses, book group accommodations, use loyalty programs for travel, and stick to a detailed budget.

FAQ 3: How can I handle last-minute venue cancellations?

Always have backup plans in place, such as alternative venues or flexible travel arrangements. Work closely with your booking agent to find solutions quickly.

FAQ 4: What should I include in my tour budget?

Your tour budget should include expenses for travel, accommodations, food, equipment, insurance, and contingency funds for unexpected costs.

FAQ 5: How can I maintain my team's health and well-being on tour?

Schedule rest days, encourage healthy eating, regular exercise, and adequate sleep, and provide mental health support when needed.

Best Practices for a Successful Sound Check

A thorough sound check is essential for ensuring that your performance or recording session runs smoothly. It allows you to identify and resolve any audio issues before they become problems during your performance. Whether you're preparing for a live show or a recording session, following these best practices for a successful sound check will help you achieve the best possible sound.

1. Arrive Early and Be Prepared

- TIMING: ARRIVE AT the venue or studio well before the scheduled start time to allow ample time for setup and troubleshooting. Rushing through a sound check increases the likelihood of missing crucial details.
    - Preparation: Bring all necessary equipment, including instruments, microphones, cables, and any personal gear like pedals or stands. Ensure everything is in working order before the sound check begins.

2. Communicate with the Sound Engineer

- INTRODUCTION: INTRODUCE yourself to the sound engineer and discuss any specific requirements or preferences you have for your sound.
    - Feedback: Provide clear feedback during the sound check, but also be open to the engineer's suggestions. They are there to help you achieve the best sound possible.

3. Start with a Line Check

- CHECK EACH INPUT: Begin by checking each input individually (microphones, instruments, etc.). Ensure that every channel is receiving a clear signal and that there are no issues like crackling cables or faulty connections.
    - Level Setting: Set the initial levels for each channel, making sure that nothing is too quiet or too loud. This will provide a solid foundation for the rest of the sound check.

4. Balance the Mix

- GROUP SOUND CHECK: After the line check, have the entire band or ensemble play together to balance the overall mix. Ensure that no single instrument or vocal overpowers the others.
    - Volume Levels: Pay attention to the volume levels between instruments and vocals. The goal is to create a balanced mix where every element is clearly heard.

5. Monitor Placement and Levels

- MONITOR PLACEMENT: Ensure that stage monitors are positioned correctly so that each performer can hear themselves and the other instruments clearly.
    - Monitor Levels: Adjust the levels in the monitors according to each performer's needs. This is crucial for ensuring that everyone can perform confidently without straining to hear.

6. Test Different Sections of the Performance

- QUIET AND LOUD SECTIONS: Test both the quietest and loudest parts of your set to ensure that the sound remains clear and balanced throughout. This helps prevent surprises during the actual performance.

- Special Effects: If you're using any effects, like reverb or delay, test them during the sound check to make sure they're set up correctly and won't cause any issues during the performance.

7. Check for Feedback

- MICROPHONE FEEDBACK: Test each microphone for feedback by walking around the stage with the mic turned on. Adjust the placement, gain, or EQ settings to eliminate any potential feedback issues.

- Speaker Placement: Ensure that the speakers are positioned to minimize the chance of feedback. Angle them away from microphones and reflective surfaces like walls.

8. Test the Room Acoustics

- ROOM SOUND: PAY ATTENTION to how the room itself affects the sound. Large, empty rooms might create echoes, while smaller, crowded spaces might absorb too much sound. Adjust your levels and EQ to compensate for the room's acoustics.

- Audience Simulation: If possible, simulate the presence of an audience (e.g., by placing some people in the room) to get a more accurate sense of how the sound will behave when the venue is full.

9. Final Walkthrough

- STAGE CHECK: WALK around the stage and listen from different positions to ensure that the sound is consistent throughout. This helps catch any anomalies that might not be noticeable from a single location.

- Final Adjustments: Make any final adjustments to the mix, monitor levels, or EQ settings based on what you hear during the walkthrough.

10. Document the Settings

- TAKE NOTES: DOCUMENT the settings for each channel, including gain, EQ, effects, and monitor levels. This is particularly important if you'll be performing multiple shows or sessions in the same venue.
    - Save the Mix: If you're using a digital mixing console, save the mix settings so they can be recalled easily for future performances.

Conclusion

A SUCCESSFUL SOUND check sets the stage for a smooth and professional performance. By arriving early, communicating effectively, and thoroughly testing your equipment, you can identify and resolve any issues before they become a problem. Remember, a well-executed sound check is not just about technical adjustments—it's about creating an environment where you can perform confidently, knowing that your sound will be the best it can be.

Developing Your Music Brand: A Step-by-Step Guide

In today's dynamic music industry, where artists are not just musicians but also brands, building and maintaining a strong brand identity is crucial. Whether you're an emerging artist or an established name, your brand sets you apart, tells your story, and connects you with your audience on a deeper level. However, navigating the complexities of music branding can be challenging, particularly when it comes to solving identity and consistency issues. This blog post explores these challenges and offers strategies to help you develop a strong and cohesive music brand.

Understanding Music Branding

MUSIC BRANDING IS THE process of crafting and communicating an artist's identity, values, and message through various elements such as visuals, sound, and public persona. A well-defined brand helps artists establish a unique presence in the market, making them recognizable and memorable to fans and industry professionals alike.

Your brand is more than just your music; it's the overall experience you offer. It includes your visual style, social media presence, public image, and even the way you interact with your audience. To develop a strong brand, you must first understand who you are as an artist and what you want to convey.

Identity Challenges in Music Branding

ONE OF THE FIRST CHALLENGES artists face is defining their brand identity. This process involves deep self-reflection and understanding of your unique qualities, influences, and the message you want to share with the world.

1. Defining Your Core Message:

Your core message is the foundation of your brand. It's what you stand for and what you want your audience to take away from your music. This message should be authentic and resonate with your personal experiences and beliefs. However, articulating this message can be difficult, especially when trying to balance artistic expression with market demands.

2. Navigating Genre Expectations:

Many artists struggle with the tension between staying true to their artistic identity and meeting the expectations of their genre or target audience. It's important to find a balance where you can express your individuality while still fitting into a recognizable genre framework.

3. Evolving Without Losing Identity:

As artists grow and evolve, their brand must adapt. However, maintaining a consistent identity throughout these changes is challenging. Your brand should be flexible enough to accommodate growth, yet stable enough to retain the core elements that define you.

Consistency Challenges in Music Branding

ONCE YOU'VE ESTABLISHED your brand identity, the next challenge is maintaining consistency across all platforms and interactions. Consistency helps reinforce your brand in the minds of your audience, making it easier for them to recognize and connect with you.

1. Visual and Aesthetic Consistency:

Your visual identity, including logos, album artwork, stage design, and merchandise, should be cohesive. Every visual element should reflect your brand's core message and aesthetic. Inconsistencies in visuals can confuse your audience and dilute your brand's impact.

2. Consistent Messaging Across Platforms:

Whether it's on social media, in interviews, or during live performances, your messaging should be consistent. This includes your tone of voice, the themes you discuss, and how you interact with fans. Inconsistent messaging can lead to a disconnect between you and your audience.

3. Managing Multiple Channels:

In today's digital age, artists are expected to maintain a presence across various platforms such as Instagram, Twitter, YouTube, and streaming services. Ensuring consistency across these channels can be challenging, especially when each platform has its unique requirements and audience.

Strategies for Developing a Strong Music Brand

TO OVERCOME IDENTITY and consistency challenges, artists can implement several strategies to build a strong and lasting brand.

1. Clarify Your Vision:

Take the time to define your vision and core message. What do you want to be known for? What impact do you want your music to have? Your vision should be the guiding principle for all your branding decisions.

2. Create a Brand Style Guide:

Develop a comprehensive style guide that outlines your visual and verbal identity. This guide should include color schemes, fonts, logo usage, and guidelines for tone and messaging. A style guide ensures consistency across all platforms and materials.

3. Be Authentic:

Authenticity is key to connecting with your audience. Be true to yourself and your experiences. Your audience can sense when you're being genuine, and this builds trust and loyalty.

4. Adapt While Staying True to Your Core:

As you evolve, allow your brand to adapt, but always stay true to your core identity. For example, if your music style changes, ensure that the change aligns with your overall brand message and doesn't alienate your existing audience.

5. Engage with Your Audience:

Building a strong brand is not just about broadcasting your message; it's also about listening to and engaging with your audience. Understand their needs and preferences, and find ways to connect with them on a personal level.

Conclusion

MUSIC BRANDING IS A powerful tool that can elevate your career and set you apart in a crowded industry. By overcoming identity and consistency challenges, you can develop a strong, authentic, and cohesive brand that resonates with your audience and withstands the test of time. Remember, your brand is an extension of who you are as an artist—make it as unique and compelling as your music.

Designing and Selling Merch That Sells

In today's music industry, selling merchandise is more than just a way to make extra money; it's a powerful tool for connecting with your fans and enhancing your brand. Music merchandise can create lasting memories, provide fans with tangible pieces of their favorite artists, and offer an additional revenue stream that supports your musical endeavors. But with so much merch out there, how do you design and sell products that truly resonate with your audience? This guide will walk you through the key strategies for creating and selling music merch that sells.

Understanding Your Audience

BEFORE DIVING INTO design and production, it's crucial to understand who you're creating merch for. Knowing your audience is the foundation of a successful merch line.

Identifying Your Fan Base

Start by identifying the demographics of your fan base. Are they primarily young adults, teens, or older music enthusiasts? Do they prefer casual wear or something more unique? Understanding the preferences, lifestyle, and values of your audience will help you design products that they'll be excited to purchase. Analyzing data from social media, streaming platforms, and concert attendance can provide valuable insights into your fan base.

Surveying Fans for Ideas

One of the best ways to ensure your merch will sell is to ask your fans directly what they want. Use social media polls, email newsletters, or even in-person surveys at shows to gather feedback on potential merch ideas. Fans are often eager to share their opinions, and involving them in the process can increase their sense of connection to your brand.

Designing Merchandise That Sells

ONCE YOU HAVE A CLEAR understanding of your audience, it's time to start designing. Your merch should not only represent your music and brand but also appeal to the tastes and preferences of your fans.

Creating Unique and Memorable Designs

Originality is key when it comes to merch design. Fans are more likely to purchase items that feel unique and exclusive to your brand. Consider collaborating with graphic designers or artists who understand your aesthetic and can help bring your ideas to life. If you prefer a more hands-on approach, there are many design tools available that allow you to create your own designs. Remember, the goal is to create something that fans will be proud to wear or display.

Incorporating Band Logos and Artwork

Your band's logo is a powerful branding tool, and incorporating it into your merch is a great way to create a sense of identity and cohesion across your products. However, don't rely solely on your logo; consider integrating other visual elements, such as album artwork, tour themes, or song lyrics. This adds depth and variety to your merch line, making each item feel special and connected to your music.

Choosing the Right Merchandise Items

When it comes to selecting merchandise items, variety is important, but so is relevance. T-shirts, hoodies, and hats are staples of any merch line, but don't be afraid to think outside the box. Depending on your audience, you might consider items like tote bags, posters, vinyl records, or even custom accessories like pins or patches. The key is to offer items that your fans will actually use and enjoy.

Merchandising Strategies for Success

DESIGNING GREAT MERCH is only half the battle; the next step is to implement strategies that will help your products sell.

Offering Limited Edition Items

Creating a sense of urgency can drive sales. Limited edition items, such as tour-specific merch or special collaborations, can entice fans to make a purchase before it's too late. Announce these items with a countdown or a limited window of availability to create excitement and anticipation.

Bundling Products for Higher Sales

Bundling is an effective strategy to increase the perceived value of your products and encourage fans to buy more. For example, you could offer a bundle that includes a t-shirt, a poster, and a digital download of your latest album at a discounted price. Bundles are also a great way to move less popular items by pairing them with best-sellers.

Pricing Your Merchandise Effectively

Pricing can make or break your merch sales. Price too high, and you might alienate potential buyers; price too low, and you might not cover your costs or devalue your brand. When setting prices, consider your production costs, the perceived value of the items, and the average price points of similar products in the market. Offering a range of price points can also help cater to different segments of your audience.

Selling Your Merchandise

WITH YOUR DESIGNS AND strategies in place, it's time to start selling. Whether online or in person, the way you present and promote your merch can significantly impact sales.

Setting Up an Online Store

An online store is a must-have for any artist looking to sell merch. Platforms like Shopify, Bandcamp, and Big Cartel offer user-friendly options for setting up and managing an online store. Ensure your store is easy to navigate, with clear product descriptions, high-quality images, and a straightforward checkout process. Consider offering different payment options and shipping methods to accommodate a wider range of customers.

Selling Merch at Live Shows

Live shows are prime opportunities to sell merch, as fans are often excited and eager to take home a souvenir. Make sure your merch table is well-organized, with items clearly displayed and easy to access. Assign a dedicated person to handle sales so you can focus on performing and interacting with fans. Offering exclusive tour merch or discounts for on-the-spot purchases can also boost sales.

Using Social Media for Merch Sales

Social media is a powerful tool for promoting your merch. Announce new products, limited editions, or sales on platforms like Instagram, Facebook, and Twitter. Use high-quality photos and engaging captions to capture attention. You can also leverage social media features like Instagram Shopping or Facebook Shops to make it easier for fans to purchase directly through your posts.

Maximizing Merchandising Profits

TO ENSURE YOUR MERCH efforts are profitable, it's important to manage costs, inventory, and production efficiently.

Managing Inventory and Costs

Keeping track of your inventory is crucial to avoid overselling or running out of popular items. Use inventory management software to monitor stock levels and sales trends. When it comes to production, aim for a balance between quality and cost. While it's tempting to go for the cheapest option, remember that low-quality merch can reflect poorly on your brand and lead to dissatisfied customers.

Expanding Your Merch Line Over Time

As your fan base grows, so should your merch line. Introduce new products gradually to keep your offerings fresh and exciting. Pay attention to what sells well and consider expanding those categories. For instance, if your t-shirts are a hit, you might experiment with different designs, colors, or styles.

Collaborating with Other Artists or Brands

Collaborations can add value and excitement to your merch line. Partnering with other artists, designers, or even brands can lead to unique and highly sought-after products. Collaborations not only expand your reach but also offer opportunities for creative cross-promotion.

Conclusion

DESIGNING AND SELLING music merchandise is both an art and a science. By understanding your audience, creating appealing designs, implementing smart merchandising strategies, and effectively selling your products, you can turn your merch into a powerful tool for fan engagement and revenue generation. Start small, stay true to your brand, and always listen to your fans. With time and effort, your merch can become a key component of your musical career.

FAQs

1. HOW DO I KNOW WHAT type of merch my fans will like?

- Start by analyzing your fan demographics and gathering direct feedback through surveys and social media polls. Understanding their preferences will guide your design choices.

2. What are the best platforms for selling music merchandise online?

- Popular platforms include Shopify, Bandcamp, and Big Cartel. Each offers unique features, so choose one that best suits your needs for ease of use, customization, and integration.

3. How can I promote my merch without feeling too salesy?

- Engage your fans by sharing behind-the-scenes content, stories about the design process, and limited-time offers. Authenticity and transparency go a long way in building trust and excitement.

4. Is it better to produce merch in-house or use a third-party service?

- It depends on your resources and goals. In-house production offers control and potentially higher margins, while third-party services can handle logistics and scale more easily.

5. How do I handle shipping and fulfillment for online orders?

- Consider using fulfillment services like Printful or ShipStation to manage shipping efficiently. They can help streamline the process, allowing you to focus on creating and promoting your merch.

Touring Tips for Beginners: A Guide for Musicians Hitting the Road

Embarking on your first tour as a musician is an exciting milestone, but it can also be daunting if you're not prepared. Touring involves more than just playing gigs; it requires careful planning, adaptability, and stamina. Whether you're hitting the road for a few local shows or embarking on a cross-country adventure, these beginner touring tips will help you navigate the challenges of touring and make the most of your experience.

1. Plan Your Route Wisely

One of the most important aspects of touring is planning your route. Consider the geography of your tour stops to minimize travel time and expenses. Try to book gigs in a logical sequence, moving from one city to the next without unnecessary backtracking. Use mapping tools and apps to plan the most efficient routes, and be sure to account for factors like traffic and road conditions.

2. Budget for All Expenses

Touring can be expensive, so it's crucial to create a detailed budget before you hit the road. Factor in costs for gas, accommodations, food, equipment maintenance, and any unforeseen expenses. It's also a good idea to have an emergency fund in case something unexpected happens. Keep track of your spending throughout the tour to stay within your budget.

3. Pack Smart and Light

Space is often limited when touring, especially if you're traveling in a van or a small vehicle. Pack only the essentials, including your instruments, gear, merchandise, and personal items. Make sure your equipment is in good working order and pack spare strings, batteries, cables, and other necessities. Use packing cubes or organizers to keep things tidy and easily accessible.

4. Prioritize Self-Care

Touring can be physically and mentally demanding, so it's important to prioritize self-care. Get enough sleep, stay hydrated, and eat nutritious meals to keep your energy levels up. Take breaks during long drives to stretch and rest. Also, make time for relaxation and downtime to recharge between performances.

5. Promote Your Shows

Promotion is key to a successful tour. Use social media, email newsletters, and your website to announce your tour dates and encourage fans to attend. Collaborate with local musicians or influencers in each city to help spread the word. Consider reaching out to local press for coverage or radio interviews to boost visibility.

6. Build Relationships with Venues and Promoters

The relationships you build with venues and promoters can have a lasting impact on your touring career. Be professional, punctual, and communicative. Show appreciation for the staff and promoters, and always fulfill your commitments. Building a reputation as a reliable and easy-to-work-with artist can lead to future opportunities.

7. Engage with Fans

Touring is a great opportunity to connect with your fans in person. Take the time to meet and interact with them before and after your shows. Sign merchandise, take photos, and express your gratitude for their support. Building strong relationships with your fans can lead to a more loyal following and better turnouts at future shows.

8. Stay Organized

Touring involves juggling a lot of details, from show times to accommodation arrangements. Use a tour itinerary or a mobile app to keep track of important information like load-in times, set times, addresses, and contact details. Staying organized will help reduce stress and ensure that everything runs smoothly.

9. Be Prepared for the Unexpected

No matter how well you plan, things don't always go according to schedule. Equipment might break, gigs might get canceled, or you might face bad weather. Stay flexible and be ready to adapt to unexpected challenges. Having a positive attitude and a backup plan can help you navigate these situations with ease.

10. Document Your Tour

Documenting your tour is not only a way to create lasting memories but also a valuable tool for connecting with your fans. Take photos, record videos, and share behind-the-scenes moments on social media. Consider keeping a tour diary or blog to share your experiences with your audience. This content can also be used for future promotional materials.

11. Learn from Each Experience

Every tour is a learning experience. After each show, take some time to reflect on what went well and what could be improved. Gather feedback from your bandmates, crew, and fans to help refine your performance and logistics. Continuous improvement will make future tours even more successful.

Final Thoughts

TOURING AS A BEGINNER can be both exhilarating and challenging, but with the right preparation and mindset, it can also be one of the most rewarding experiences of your musical journey. By planning ahead, staying organized, and taking care of yourself and your team, you'll be better equipped to handle the ups and downs of life on the road. Most importantly, enjoy the ride and make the most of every opportunity to share your music with new audiences.

Understanding Microphone Feedback and How to Avoid It

Microphone feedback is one of the most common and frustrating issues faced by musicians, speakers, and audio engineers. That high-pitched screech or loud hum can disrupt a performance, irritate the audience, and leave you scrambling to fix the problem. Fortunately, by understanding the causes of microphone feedback and implementing a few strategies, you can significantly reduce or eliminate it altogether.

What is Microphone Feedback?

MICROPHONE FEEDBACK occurs when a microphone picks up sound from a speaker that is amplified and sent back through the speaker again, creating a loop. This loop amplifies the sound repeatedly, resulting in the unpleasant noise known as feedback.

Common Causes of Microphone Feedback

1. PROXIMITY OF MICROPHONE to Speaker: The closer the microphone is to the speaker, the more likely it is to pick up sound from the speaker and create a feedback loop.

2. Microphone Gain: If the gain (sensitivity) on the microphone is too high, it will pick up more sound from its surroundings, increasing the chances of feedback.

3. Poor Room Acoustics: Certain environments, especially those with reflective surfaces, can cause sound to bounce around and increase the likelihood of feedback.

4. Improper Speaker Placement: If speakers are positioned in such a way that they project sound directly towards the microphone, feedback is more likely to occur.

How to Avoid Microphone Feedback

1. POSITION YOUR MICROPHONE and Speakers Strategically: Keep microphones as far away from speakers as possible and avoid pointing the microphone directly at any speakers. Angling speakers away from the microphone and towards the audience can help prevent feedback.

2. Lower the Microphone Gain: Reduce the gain on your microphone to minimize the amount of ambient sound it picks up. You want the microphone to capture your voice or instrument clearly, without picking up unnecessary background noise.

3. Use a Directional Microphone: Directional microphones, such as cardioid or supercardioid mics, are designed to pick up sound from a specific direction. This helps to reduce the likelihood of feedback by minimizing the amount of sound the microphone picks up from the speakers or other sources.

4. Utilize EQ to Cut Problem Frequencies: Feedback often occurs at specific frequencies. By using an equalizer (EQ) to identify and reduce those frequencies, you can prevent feedback. A technique known as "notching" involves cutting the frequency bands where feedback is most likely to occur.

5. Use a Feedback Eliminator: Feedback eliminators are devices or software that automatically detect and suppress feedback frequencies. They can be particularly useful in complex audio setups or environments prone to feedback.

6. Adjust the Room Acoustics: If possible, improve the acoustics of the room where you're performing. Adding sound-absorbing materials

like curtains, carpets, or acoustic panels can help reduce reflections and the likelihood of feedback.

7. Monitor Levels Carefully: Keep an eye on the levels of your audio equipment, including the microphone, mixer, and speakers. Ensure that no single component is overly amplified, as this can contribute to feedback.

8. Perform a Sound Check: Before your performance, always conduct a thorough sound check to identify any potential feedback issues. Walk around the space with the microphone to see if any areas are particularly prone to feedback, and make adjustments as needed.

Conclusion

MICROPHONE FEEDBACK is a common challenge, but with the right techniques, it can be managed effectively. By positioning your equipment strategically, adjusting settings, and using the right tools, you can minimize the chances of feedback and ensure a smooth performance. Remember, a little preparation goes a long way in creating a professional and pleasant audio experience for both you and your audience.

Essential Monitor EQ Tips: Equalizing Onstage Monitors For Clear Sound

Properly Equalizing your onstage monitors is crucial for ensuring that you and your fellow performers can hear everything clearly during a live performance. When your monitor mix is well-balanced, you can focus on your performance without straining to hear yourself or other band members. Here are some essential tips for EQing your monitors to achieve optimal sound on stage.

1. Start with a Flat EQ

- Baseline Settings: Begin with all EQ settings flat (no boosts or cuts). This gives you a neutral starting point from which you can make adjustments based on the specific needs of the stage and performers.

- Adjust Incrementally: Make small, gradual adjustments to the EQ. Large changes can cause drastic shifts in sound, which can be disorienting and difficult to control.

2. Tackle Feedback First

- Identify Problem Frequencies: Feedback often occurs at specific frequencies. Use a parametric EQ to narrow in on the feedback frequency and then reduce it with a notch filter.

- High-Pass Filters: Engage a high-pass filter to remove low-end rumble and sub-bass frequencies that can muddy the monitor mix and contribute to feedback. Set the filter around 80-100 Hz, depending on the instrument or vocal.

3. Enhance Clarity

- Cut Muddy Frequencies: In the low-mid range (around 200-500 Hz), excessive energy can cause the mix to sound muddy. Gently cut these frequencies to clear up the sound, especially for vocals and guitars.

- Boost Presence: To improve clarity and definition, especially for vocals, slightly boost the presence range (around 2-5 kHz). This helps the vocals cut through the mix without being overpowering.

4. Balance the High Frequencies

- Avoid Harshness: High frequencies (above 10 kHz) can sometimes be harsh or piercing in monitors. If the sound is too bright or sibilant, slightly reduce these frequencies to create a smoother, more comfortable listening experience.

- Cymbals and High-Hats: For drummers, ensure that cymbals and hi-hats are clear but not overpowering in the mix. A subtle boost around 10 kHz can add brilliance, but too much can lead to ear fatigue.

5. Customize for Each Performer

- Individual Preferences: Every performer has different preferences for their monitor mix. Some may need more bass, while others might require more midrange or treble. Tailor the EQ for each monitor to suit the specific needs of each performer.

- Instrument-Specific EQ: If monitors are dedicated to specific instruments (e.g., a monitor for the drummer or bassist), adjust the EQ to highlight the most critical frequencies for that instrument.

6. Keep the Mix Natural

- Avoid Over-EQing: While it's important to address problem areas, avoid the temptation to over-EQ. Too many cuts and boosts can result in an unnatural sound that's difficult to work with on stage.

- Maintain Tonal Balance: Ensure that the overall tonal balance of the monitor mix remains natural. The goal is to replicate the sound of the instruments and vocals as accurately as possible, with adjustments made only for clarity and feedback control.

7. Test and Adjust On Stage

- Sound Check Adjustments: After setting the initial EQ, test the sound on stage during sound check. Walk around and listen from different positions to ensure consistency in the monitor mix.

- Fine-Tuning: Use the sound check to fine-tune the EQ based on how the monitors sound in the live environment. Make adjustments in real-time and check with the performers to ensure they're comfortable with the sound.

8. Monitor the Volume

- Avoid Excessive Volume: Loud monitors can lead to hearing fatigue and make it difficult to achieve a clean mix. Keep monitor levels at a comfortable volume that allows everyone to hear clearly without overwhelming the stage sound.

- Protect Hearing: Encourage the use of in-ear monitors or earplugs for performers to protect their hearing, especially in loud environments. This can also reduce the need for excessive volume in stage monitors.

Conclusion

EQING YOUR STAGE MONITORS effectively is key to ensuring a clear, balanced, and feedback-free mix that allows performers to hear themselves and each other comfortably. By starting with a flat EQ, addressing feedback, and making careful, purposeful adjustments, you can create a monitor mix that supports a great performance. Remember, the goal is to enhance clarity while maintaining a natural sound, so performers can focus on delivering their best on stage.

Best Practices for Booking Gigs Successfully

Booking gigs is an essential part of building your music career, but it can also be one of the most challenging aspects, especially when communication with venues doesn't go smoothly. Whether it's slow responses, unclear expectations, or last-minute changes, poor communication can derail your plans and cause unnecessary stress. Here's how to troubleshoot common issues and improve your gig booking processes through better venue communication.

1. Research Before Reaching Out

BEFORE CONTACTING A venue, do your homework. Understand the type of music they typically host, their audience, and the size and layout of the space. This information will help you tailor your pitch and show that you're serious about playing there. It also ensures that the venue is a good fit for your music, saving you time and potential frustration later on.

2. Craft a Clear and Concise Pitch

YOUR INITIAL OUTREACH should be professional and to the point. Introduce yourself, describe your music, and explain why you want to play at their venue. Include links to your music, social media profiles, and any relevant press or past gig experiences. Keep it brief—venue managers are busy and appreciate clear, concise communication.

Example Pitch:

"Hi [Venue Name],

I'm [Your Name], a [genre] musician from [city]. I've been following [venue's name] and believe my music would resonate with your audience. I'd love to discuss the possibility of performing at your venue. You can listen to my latest tracks [here], and see some recent live performances [here]. Let me know if you'd be interested, and we can talk details.

Looking forward to hearing from you!

Best,

[Your Name]"

3. Follow Up Respectfully

IF YOU DON'T HEAR BACK within a reasonable timeframe (usually one to two weeks), send a polite follow-up. Venue managers often receive a high volume of emails, and a respectful nudge can help your message stand out without coming off as pushy.

Example Follow-Up:

"Hi [Venue Name],

I wanted to follow up on my previous email about performing at your venue. I'm very interested in the opportunity and would love to discuss it further if you have the time. I've included the original email below for your reference.

Thanks again for considering my request!

Best,

[Your Name]"

4. Be Clear About Expectations

ONCE YOU'VE ESTABLISHED contact, it's important to be clear about expectations from both sides. Discuss details like the date and time of the gig, payment, soundcheck times, load-in/load-out procedures, and any technical requirements. Putting everything in writing helps avoid misunderstandings and ensures that both you and the venue are on the same page.

5. Be Responsive and Professional

TIMELY COMMUNICATION is key to maintaining a good relationship with venues. Respond promptly to emails and messages, and be professional in all your interactions. If you have any concerns or need clarification, don't hesitate to ask, but always do so respectfully.

6. Prepare for Last-Minute Changes

EVEN WITH THE BEST planning, last-minute changes can happen. Venues might adjust set times, or there could be unforeseen technical issues. Stay flexible and have backup plans when possible. Maintaining a calm and professional demeanor in these situations shows the venue that you're reliable and easy to work with, increasing your chances of being booked again in the future.

7. Confirm Details in Advance

A DAY OR TWO BEFORE the gig, send a confirmation email to the venue to ensure everything is set. Confirm the time, address, and any other important details. This not only shows professionalism but also helps avoid any last-minute surprises.

Example Confirmation Email:

"Hi [Venue Name],

I'm excited about the upcoming gig on [date]! I just wanted to confirm the details: [list of key details, such as set time, load-in time, and payment arrangements]. Please let me know if there are any changes or if anything else is needed from my side.

Looking forward to it!

Best,
[Your Name]"

8. Maintain Good Relationships

AFTER THE GIG, SEND a thank-you note to the venue, expressing your appreciation for the opportunity to perform. If things went well, mention your interest in playing there again. Building and maintaining good relationships with venues is crucial for securing future bookings and can lead to better opportunities down the road.

Example Thank-You Note:

"Hi [Venue Name],

Thank you so much for having me at [venue name] last night. I had a fantastic time and appreciated the opportunity to share my music with your audience. I'd love to stay in touch for any future events. Thanks again for all your support!

Best,
[Your Name]"

Conclusion

EFFECTIVE COMMUNICATION is the backbone of successful gig booking. By being clear, respectful, and professional in your interactions with venues, you can troubleshoot common issues and improve your booking process. Remember, every gig is not just an opportunity to perform, but also to build lasting relationships in the music industry. With the right approach, you'll not only secure more gigs but also create a reputation as a reliable and professional artist.

Fan Engagement Strategies for Authentic Connection

In the fast-paced, ever-evolving world of music, building a strong and loyal fanbase is more critical than ever. However, the key to not just gaining fans but keeping them engaged lies in the authenticity of your interactions. This is the art of fan engagement strategies, a puzzle that many artists struggle to solve. But fear not! With the right strategies, you can connect with your fans in a meaningful and lasting way. Here's how:

1. Know Your Audience

UNDERSTANDING YOUR audience is the first step to authentic engagement. Take the time to learn who your fans are—what they like, what they value, and how they interact online. Use analytics tools to track demographics, engagement patterns, and feedback. This information will help you tailor your content and communication style to resonate with your fans' needs and preferences.

2. Be Genuine in Your Communication

FANS CAN TELL WHEN an artist is being inauthentic. Whether you're posting on social media, responding to comments, or engaging in live streams, make sure your interactions are sincere. Share your true thoughts, experiences, and feelings. Authenticity builds trust, and trust fosters loyalty.

3. Share Behind-the-Scenes Content

PEOPLE LOVE GETTING a peek behind the curtain. Share snippets of your life as an artist—whether it's the creative process, rehearsals, or just a day in the life. This kind of content makes fans feel like they're part of your journey, deepening their connection to you and your music.

4. Respond to Your Fans

ONE OF THE MOST EFFECTIVE ways to engage with your fans is by acknowledging them. Reply to comments, like posts where you're tagged, and show appreciation for fan art or covers. Even a simple "thank you" can make a fan feel valued and more connected to you.

5. Host Interactive Events

LIVE STREAMS, Q&A SESSIONS, and virtual meet-and-greets are fantastic ways to engage directly with your fans. These events create a two-way conversation, allowing you to interact with your audience in real-time. They also provide an opportunity for fans to ask questions, offer feedback, and feel more involved in your journey.

6. Incorporate Fan Feedback

LISTENING TO YOUR FANS and incorporating their feedback shows that you value their opinions. Whether it's about a new song, a piece of merch, or even tour locations, taking their suggestions into account can make them feel like they're part of the creative process.

7. Create a Community

BUILDING A COMMUNITY around your music is a powerful way to keep fans engaged. Encourage fans to connect with each other through your social media platforms, fan clubs, or online forums. A strong, connected fan community can sustain itself, with fans keeping each other excited and engaged, even when you're not actively promoting something.

8. Give Back to Your Fans

OFFER EXCLUSIVE CONTENT, early access to new music, or limited-edition merchandise as a way to reward your most loyal fans. These gestures of appreciation can go a long way in building a dedicated fanbase. Moreover, when fans feel appreciated, they're more likely to stick around and continue supporting your career.

9. Be Consistent

CONSISTENCY IS KEY to maintaining fan engagement. Regular updates, consistent communication, and ongoing interaction keep your fans invested. Whether you're releasing new music, sharing updates, or simply interacting on social media, make sure you're consistent in your presence and engagement.

10. Stay True to Your Art

LASTLY, NEVER LOSE sight of your music and what makes you unique. Fans are drawn to your authenticity and creativity, so stay true to your artistic vision. When your art is genuine, the connection with your fans will naturally follow.

Conclusion

SOLVING THE FAN ENGAGEMENT puzzle is not about following a rigid formula but about connecting authentically with your audience. By understanding your fans, communicating sincerely, and consistently engaging with them, you can build a loyal fanbase that grows with you throughout your career. Remember, at the heart of it all is the music and the unique bond you create with those who love it.

Effective Band Bios: Crafting Compelling Artist Stories

A well-crafted band bio is more than just a collection of facts; it's a story that captures the essence of who you are as a group and what you stand for. Whether you're a new band looking to make your mark or an established act seeking to refresh your image, a compelling band bio is crucial for connecting with fans, promoters, and industry professionals. Here's how to craft a compelling artist story that resonates.

1. Know Your Audience

BEFORE YOU START WRITING, consider who will be reading your bio. Are you targeting fans, press, venue owners, or record labels? Each audience might be looking for something slightly different, so tailor your bio to meet their needs.

Tip: For a general band bio, aim for a balance that appeals to all potential readers. If you're writing for a specific purpose, such as submitting to a festival, emphasize elements that align with that event's vibe or audience.

2. Start with a Strong Hook

THE OPENING OF YOUR bio should grab the reader's attention. Think of it as the first impression you make on someone who knows nothing about your band. A compelling hook could be an intriguing fact, a memorable quote, or a bold statement about your music.

Example: "Born in the heart of the city and raised on the raw energy of the underground scene, [Band Name] delivers a sonic experience that's as gritty as it is exhilarating."

3. Tell Your Story

EVERY BAND HAS A STORY, and this is the heart of your bio. How did you come together? What drives your music? What challenges have you overcome? Your story should reflect your band's personality, values, and journey, making it relatable and engaging.

Tip: Focus on what makes your band unique. Whether it's your origin story, the diversity of your influences, or your mission as a group, highlight the elements that set you apart from other bands.

4. Highlight Key Achievements

WHILE YOUR BIO SHOULD be narrative-driven, it's also important to include your band's accomplishments. This could be anything from releasing an album, playing at notable venues, winning awards, or collaborating with other artists. These achievements lend credibility and show that you're serious about your craft.

Tip: Be selective and concise. Highlight the most impressive and relevant achievements without overwhelming the reader with too much information.

5. Describe Your Sound

YOUR MUSIC IS, OF COURSE, the core of your band's identity. But describing music can be tricky, especially if your sound doesn't fit neatly into a single genre. Use vivid, descriptive language to convey the essence of your sound, and don't be afraid to reference other artists or genres to give readers a point of reference.

Example: "With soaring vocals, intricate guitar work, and a rhythm section that grooves like no other, [Band Name] blends the anthemic energy of classic rock with the introspective depth of indie folk."

6. Show Your Personality

YOUR BIO IS AN OPPORTUNITY to show off your band's personality. Whether you're edgy and rebellious, laid-back and fun, or deeply introspective, let that shine through in your writing. This helps to create a connection with readers who share similar vibes or values.

Tip: Incorporate humor, wit, or emotion where appropriate, but keep it authentic. Forced humor or exaggerated claims can come off as insincere.

7. Keep It Concise and Readable

ATTENTION SPANS ARE short, especially in today's digital age. Your band bio should be engaging but also to the point. Aim for a length of around 250-400 words for a standard bio. Use short paragraphs, bullet points, or headings to break up the text and make it more digestible.

Tip: After writing your bio, step away from it for a bit, then return with fresh eyes to edit and trim any unnecessary details. Make sure every word serves a purpose.

8. Include a Call to Action

WHILE THE PRIMARY PURPOSE of your bio is to inform and engage, it's also a good idea to direct readers to where they can hear your music, follow you on social media, or get in touch for bookings. A simple call to action at the end of your bio can guide them to the next step.

Example: "Check out [Band Name]'s latest single on Spotify, and follow them on Instagram for updates on new releases and upcoming shows."

Final Thoughts

CRAFTING AN EFFECTIVE band bio is both an art and a science. It requires a balance of storytelling, factual information, and personality to create a narrative that truly represents your band. Remember, your bio is often the first impression someone will have of your group, so make it count. With these tips in mind, you can create a compelling artist story that resonates with your audience and leaves a lasting impression.

Fan Feedback: Handling Criticism and Building Resilience

As a musician, fan feedback is an inevitable part of your journey. Whether it's praise for your latest release or constructive criticism of a live performance, how you handle feedback can significantly impact your growth as an artist and your relationship with your audience. While positive comments are always welcome, it's the negative or critical feedback that often challenges your confidence and resilience. This blog post explores how to manage fan feedback constructively, handle criticism gracefully, and build the resilience needed to thrive in the music industry.

The Importance of Fan Feedback

FAN FEEDBACK IS A VALUABLE resource for musicians. It provides insight into how your music resonates with your audience and can guide your creative decisions. Here's why it's important to pay attention to what your fans are saying:

1. Understanding Audience Preferences:

Feedback helps you understand what your fans love about your music and what they might want more (or less) of. This can inform your future projects and help you stay connected to your audience's evolving tastes.

2. Personal and Professional Growth:

Constructive criticism offers an opportunity for growth. It highlights areas where you can improve and challenges you to refine your craft, making you a better musician.

3. Strengthening Fan Relationships:

Engaging with fan feedback—whether positive or negative—shows that you value your audience's opinions. This interaction can strengthen your connection with fans and foster a loyal community around your music.

Handling Criticism Gracefully

CRITICISM CAN BE DIFFICULT to accept, especially when you've put your heart and soul into your work. However, how you respond to criticism can either build or undermine your credibility as an artist. Here's how to handle criticism gracefully:

1. Separate Yourself from Your Work

It's important to remember that criticism of your music is not a personal attack. Your art is an expression of your creativity, but it doesn't define your worth as a person. By distancing yourself from your work, you can evaluate feedback more objectively.

- Don't Take It Personally: Understand that not everyone will connect with your music in the same way. Negative feedback is often a reflection of personal taste rather than a judgment of your talent.

- Focus on the Message, Not the Tone: Sometimes criticism is delivered harshly. Instead of reacting to the tone, try to extract the constructive elements of the feedback. What can you learn from it?

2. Respond with Gratitude

When faced with criticism, your first instinct might be to defend yourself or dismiss the feedback. Instead, take a moment to express gratitude.

- Thank the Critic: A simple "Thank you for your feedback" can go a long way. It shows that you are open to different perspectives and willing to engage in a constructive dialogue.

- Acknowledge Valid Points: If the criticism is valid, acknowledge it. For example, if a fan points out a flaw in your performance, you might say, "I appreciate you bringing this to my attention, and I'll work on improving that aspect."

3. Reflect Before Responding

It's natural to feel defensive when receiving criticism, but responding impulsively can lead to unnecessary conflict. Instead, take time to reflect on the feedback before you respond.

- Pause and Breathe: If you're feeling upset, take a break before responding. This gives you time to calm down and approach the situation with a clear mind.

- Consider the Source: Not all criticism is equally valuable. Consider the source of the feedback—are they a long-time fan, a fellow musician, or someone with little knowledge of your genre? This can help you decide how much weight to give their opinion.

4. Engage Constructively

Engaging constructively with critics can turn a negative situation into a positive one. It can lead to meaningful conversations that benefit both you and your fans.

- Ask for Specifics: If the criticism is vague, ask for more details. For example, if someone says they didn't like a song, you could ask, "What specifically didn't work for you?" This can provide you with actionable insights.

- Offer Your Perspective: While it's important to listen, it's also okay to share your perspective. You might explain your artistic choices or the context behind a particular decision. Just be sure to do so respectfully and without sounding defensive.

Building Resilience in the Face of Criticism

DEVELOPING RESILIENCE is crucial for long-term success in the music industry. Resilience allows you to bounce back from setbacks, maintain your passion for music, and continue growing as an artist. Here's how to build resilience when dealing with criticism:

1. Embrace a Growth Mindset

A growth mindset is the belief that your abilities and talents can be developed through effort and learning. This mindset helps you view criticism as an opportunity for improvement rather than a threat.

- See Criticism as Feedback, Not Failure: Instead of viewing criticism as a reflection of your shortcomings, see it as valuable feedback that can help you grow.

- Learn from Mistakes: Mistakes are an inevitable part of the creative process. Embrace them as learning opportunities and use them to refine your skills.

2. Surround Yourself with Support

Having a strong support system can help you stay grounded and resilient in the face of criticism.

- Seek Out Constructive Critique: Surround yourself with people who give you honest, constructive feedback. This could be fellow musicians, mentors, or trusted friends. Their input can help you improve without feeling discouraged.

- Lean on Your Community: When you're feeling down about negative feedback, reach out to your community of supporters. Their encouragement can remind you of your strengths and keep you motivated.

3. Focus on Your Vision

It's important to stay true to your artistic vision, even when faced with criticism. Remember why you started making music and what you want to achieve.

- Set Personal Goals: Set goals that align with your vision and measure your success by your own standards, not by the opinions of others.

- Stay Passionate: Keep your passion for music alive by focusing on the aspects of your work that bring you joy. Passion fuels resilience and helps you push through challenges.

4. Practice Self-Care

Taking care of your mental and emotional well-being is essential for building resilience.

- Take Breaks: If criticism is overwhelming, it's okay to take a step back and focus on self-care. Spend time doing things you enjoy outside of music to recharge your energy.

- Develop Healthy Coping Strategies: Find healthy ways to cope with stress and criticism, such as exercise, meditation, or talking to a therapist. These strategies can help you maintain a positive mindset.

Conclusion

FAN FEEDBACK IS AN integral part of your journey as a musician. While criticism can be challenging, handling it with grace and building resilience can help you grow as an artist and strengthen your connection with your audience. By embracing a growth mindset, surrounding yourself with support, staying true to your vision, and practicing self-care, you can navigate feedback constructively and continue to thrive in your musical career. Remember, every piece of feedback—positive or negative—is an opportunity to learn, grow, and become the best version of yourself as an artist.

Live Performance Anxiety: Techniques for Overcoming Stage Fright

For many musicians, the thrill of performing live is accompanied by an unwelcome companion—stage fright. This anxiety can manifest as a racing heart, shaky hands, dry mouth, or even an overwhelming sense of dread. While some nerves can be beneficial, giving you the energy and focus to perform at your best, too much anxiety can hinder your ability to deliver a great performance. The good news is that stage fright is manageable. In this post, we'll explore techniques to help you overcome live performance anxiety and take control of your nerves.

Understanding Stage Fright

STAGE FRIGHT, OR PERFORMANCE anxiety, is a common experience among musicians, regardless of their level of experience. It's a natural response to the pressure of performing in front of an audience. This anxiety often stems from the fear of making mistakes, being judged, or not meeting one's own expectations.

The physical symptoms of stage fright are triggered by the body's "fight or flight" response, which releases adrenaline to prepare you for perceived danger. While this response is helpful in truly dangerous situations, it can be counterproductive when you're simply trying to perform music.

Techniques for Overcoming Stage Fright

OVERCOMING STAGE FRIGHT requires a combination of mental and physical strategies. Here are some techniques to help you manage your nerves and perform with confidence:

1. Preparation is Key

One of the most effective ways to reduce performance anxiety is through thorough preparation. The more confident you are in your ability to perform the material, the less likely you are to be derailed by nerves.

- Practice Regularly: Rehearse your set until you can perform it smoothly, even under pressure. Break down difficult sections and practice them repeatedly.

- Simulate Performance Conditions: Practice in environments that mimic live performance settings. Play in front of friends or record yourself to get used to performing under observation.

- Know Your Material Inside and Out: The more familiar you are with your music, the more comfortable you'll feel on stage. Ensure you know every note, lyric, and transition.

2. Focus on Your Breathing

Deep, controlled breathing can help calm your nerves by reducing the physical symptoms of anxiety.

- Breathing Exercises: Practice deep breathing exercises before and during your performance. Inhale slowly through your nose, hold the breath for a few seconds, and then exhale slowly through your mouth. This can help slow your heart rate and clear your mind.

- Mindful Breathing on Stage: If you feel anxious during your performance, take a moment to focus on your breathing. Even a few deep breaths can help you regain control.

3. Visualization and Positive Imagery

Visualization is a powerful technique that can help you mentally prepare for your performance and reduce anxiety.

- Visualize Success: Close your eyes and imagine yourself performing confidently and successfully. Picture the audience enjoying your music and yourself playing without mistakes. This positive imagery can help build your confidence.

- Positive Self-Talk: Replace negative thoughts with positive affirmations. Instead of thinking, "What if I mess up?" tell yourself, "I've practiced hard and I'm ready to give a great performance."

4. Establish a Pre-Performance Routine

Having a pre-performance routine can help signal to your mind and body that it's time to perform, creating a sense of familiarity and control.

- Warm-Up Exercises: Include warm-up exercises as part of your routine, such as vocal exercises, stretching, or playing scales. This helps you physically and mentally prepare.

- Rituals for Calm: Some musicians find it helpful to have a small ritual before going on stage, like drinking a specific tea, meditating, or wearing a lucky item. Find what works for you to create a calming routine.

5. Start Small and Build Confidence

If the thought of performing in front of a large audience is overwhelming, start by performing in smaller, more comfortable settings.

- Open Mics and Small Venues: Begin with low-pressure environments like open mics, small venues, or private gatherings. These settings allow you to build confidence without the added pressure of a large audience.

- Gradually Increase Audience Size: As you become more comfortable, gradually increase the size of your audience. This step-by-step approach can help you acclimate to performing under different conditions.

6. Accept and Embrace Nervousness

It's important to acknowledge that feeling nervous before a performance is completely normal. Instead of trying to eliminate your nerves entirely, focus on managing them and turning that energy into a positive force.

- Reframe Your Anxiety: Try to view your nerves as excitement rather than fear. This shift in perspective can help you channel your energy into a dynamic performance.

- Allow Yourself to Feel: Give yourself permission to feel nervous. Accepting your anxiety rather than fighting it can reduce its intensity.

7. Connect with Your Audience

Remember that your audience is there to enjoy your music, not to judge you. Building a connection with them can help ease your nerves.

- Make Eye Contact: Engage with your audience by making eye contact. This helps create a sense of connection and reduces the feeling of being isolated on stage.

- Focus on the Music: Shift your focus from the audience's reactions to the music itself. Immerse yourself in the performance and let the music be your guide.

Conclusion

STAGE FRIGHT IS A COMMON challenge for musicians, but it doesn't have to hold you back. By implementing these techniques—preparation, breathing exercises, visualization, establishing a routine, and gradually building your confidence—you can manage your nerves and perform with greater ease. Remember, the goal isn't to eliminate stage fright but to learn how to perform despite it. With practice and patience, you can turn your anxiety into an asset, allowing you to deliver powerful and memorable performances.

Creating a Killer EPK: Essential Elements and Troubleshooting

In the music and entertainment industry, first impressions are everything, and nothing makes a better first impression than a killer Electronic Press Kit (EPK). Whether you're an emerging artist, a seasoned band, or a professional in any creative field, an EPK is your golden ticket to capturing attention, securing gigs, and elevating your brand. But what exactly goes into creating an EPK that stands out from the crowd? In this article, we'll break down the essential elements and guide you through the process of building an impressive EPK, while also troubleshooting common issues you might encounter along the way.

What is an EPK?

AN ELECTRONIC PRESS Kit, or EPK, is a digital portfolio that provides the media, booking agents, and other industry professionals with everything they need to know about you. Think of it as your online resume, but with more flair and multimedia elements that showcase your talent and personality.

In the past, artists and bands would send physical press kits to media outlets, containing printed bios, photos, and CDs. With the rise of digital media, EPKs have become the standard, allowing for instant sharing and access to your materials anytime, anywhere.

Why Do You Need a Killer EPK?

HAVING A WELL-CRAFTED EPK is crucial for several reasons:
- Professionalism: An EPK presents you as a serious artist or professional who is ready for business.

- Accessibility: It allows industry professionals to quickly access and share your information.

- Brand Building: A killer EPK helps you control your narrative and brand image.

- Time-Saving: With all your materials in one place, you save time when pitching yourself to potential clients or media outlets.

Essential Elements of an EPK

BIOGRAPHY

Your biography is the heart of your EPK. It tells your story, highlights your achievements, and gives a personal touch that connects with the reader. Whether you're an artist, band, or professional, your bio should be concise yet compelling. Include key milestones, influences, and what sets you apart in your field.

High-Quality Media

Visuals are a powerful tool in your EPK. Professional photos, album covers, and logos create a strong visual identity. If you're a musician, including video content like music videos or live performances is a must. This allows industry professionals to see and hear you in action.

Discography or Portfolio

This section is where you showcase your work. For musicians, this means listing albums, singles, and notable collaborations. If you're in another field, include a portfolio of your best projects. Organize this content in a way that's easy to navigate, making sure your most impressive work is front and center.

Press Clippings and Reviews

Positive press and reviews can add significant weight to your EPK. Include snippets of articles, interviews, and reviews that highlight your work. If you're just starting and don't have much press coverage, consider including testimonials from fans or clients.

Contact Information

Make it easy for people to reach you. Include your email, phone number, and links to your social media profiles. If you have a manager or publicist, be sure to include their contact details as well.

Tour Dates and Event Information

If you're a performing artist, this section is essential. Keep your tour dates, upcoming shows, and events up-to-date. This not only informs your audience but can also help you book more gigs by showing your active schedule.

Branding and Design

Your EPK should reflect your brand's identity. Use consistent colors, fonts, and imagery that match your other promotional materials. A well-designed EPK creates a memorable impression and sets you apart from others.

Building Your EPK: Step-by-Step Guide

CHOOSING THE RIGHT Platform

Decide whether you want a hosted EPK (on platforms like Sonicbids or ReverbNation) or a self-hosted EPK on your website. Each option has its pros and cons, depending on your needs and budget.

Designing Your EPK

Focus on creating a user-friendly layout that's easy to navigate. A clean, organized design will keep the viewer engaged. Don't forget to make your EPK mobile-responsive, as many people will view it on their phones.

Writing and Editing Content

The content in your EPK should be clear, concise, and free of errors. Write in a way that's engaging and professional. Editing is crucial – ensure everything is polished before you share your EPK with the world.

Troubleshooting Common EPK Problems

TECHNICAL ISSUES

Broken links and missing files can ruin the effectiveness of your EPK. Regularly check your EPK to ensure all links are working and files are properly uploaded.

Outdated Content

Keeping your EPK current is vital. Update it regularly with new photos, press clippings, and tour dates to reflect your latest achievements.

Lack of Engagement

If your EPK isn't generating the response you hoped for, consider adding more interactive elements like videos or links to your social media. Engaging content can make a big difference.

Conclusion

CREATING A KILLER EPK is about more than just putting together a few photos and a bio. It's about telling your story in a way that resonates with industry professionals and showcases your unique talents. By including all the essential elements and keeping your EPK up-to-date, you'll be well on your way to making a lasting impression.

FAQs

1. HOW OFTEN SHOULD I update my EPK?

- You should update your EPK whenever there's a significant change, such as a new release, tour dates, or major press coverage. Aim to review and refresh your EPK at least every few months.

2. Can I use a free platform to create my EPK?

- Yes, there are free platforms available, but they may come with limitations. A self-hosted EPK on your website offers more flexibility and control over your content and branding.

3. What should I do if I don't have any press clippings?

- If you lack press coverage, consider including testimonials from fans or industry peers. You can also focus on building this section over time as you gain more exposure.

4. How do I make my EPK stand out?

- Focus on high-quality visuals, a compelling bio, and engaging content. Make sure your EPK reflects your unique brand and personality.

5. Is it necessary to have both a website and an EPK?

- While not mandatory, having both a website and an EPK can be beneficial. Your website serves as a broader online presence, while your EPK is a targeted tool for media and industry professionals.

Live Streaming Hacks: Troubleshooting Livestream Issues

Live streaming has become a powerful tool for musicians, content creators, businesses, and anyone looking to connect with their audience in real-time. However, the success of a live stream can be quickly derailed by technical glitches. Nothing is more frustrating than buffering, poor audio quality, or sudden disconnects when you're trying to deliver a live performance or presentation. Fortunately, with the right preparation and troubleshooting livestream issues, you can minimize these issues and ensure a smooth, glitch-free live stream. Here are some essential hacks to keep your live stream running flawlessly.

1. Prepare Your Equipment and Setup

BEFORE YOU GO LIVE, it's crucial to ensure that your equipment and setup are optimized for streaming.

- Check Your Internet Connection: A strong, stable internet connection is the backbone of any live stream. Aim for an upload speed of at least 5 Mbps for standard definition streaming and 10 Mbps or higher for HD quality. Use a wired Ethernet connection instead of Wi-Fi to reduce the risk of drops in connection quality.

- Test Your Equipment: Before going live, thoroughly test your camera, microphone, and any other equipment. Ensure that your camera is producing a clear image, your microphone is capturing clean audio, and all connections are secure.

- Update Software and Firmware: Make sure that all your streaming software, camera, and audio equipment are up to date. Software updates often include bug fixes and performance improvements that can enhance your streaming experience.

2. Optimize Audio Quality

POOR AUDIO QUALITY is a major turnoff for viewers, even more so than low video quality. Here's how to ensure your sound is top-notch.

- Use an External Microphone: Built-in microphones on cameras or laptops often produce subpar audio. Invest in a good quality external microphone, whether it's a USB mic, a lavalier, or a professional condenser mic, to capture clear, crisp sound.

- Eliminate Background Noise: Stream from a quiet environment to minimize background noise. If noise is unavoidable, consider using noise-cancelling software or a microphone with a built-in noise reduction feature.

- Monitor Audio Levels: Use headphones to monitor your audio levels in real-time. This helps you catch and correct issues like clipping, distortion, or overly quiet sound before they ruin your stream.

3. Ensure Stable Video Quality

GLITCHES IN VIDEO QUALITY can distract your audience and make your stream difficult to watch.

- Adjust Bitrate Settings: Bitrate controls the quality of your video stream. If your stream is experiencing lag or buffering, consider lowering the bitrate. A lower bitrate requires less bandwidth and can help maintain a smoother stream.

- Choose the Right Resolution: Streaming at a resolution that your internet connection and equipment can't handle will result in dropped frames and poor video quality. Streaming in 720p is often a good balance between quality and stability if you're facing bandwidth limitations.

- Use a Backup Camera: If possible, have a second camera set up and ready to go in case your primary camera fails. Switching to a backup camera can save your stream if the primary camera encounters issues.

4. Optimize Your Streaming Software

YOUR STREAMING SOFTWARE is the control center for your live stream, so it's important to set it up correctly.

- Use a Reliable Streaming Platform: Whether you're using OBS, Streamlabs, or another software, make sure it's stable and well-suited to your needs. Test different platforms to see which works best with your hardware and streaming style.

- Set Up Scenes in Advance: If your stream involves multiple scenes (e.g., different camera angles, slideshows, or overlays), set them up in your streaming software beforehand. This minimizes the risk of mistakes or delays when switching between scenes during the live stream.

- Enable Stream Delay: If you're concerned about technical glitches or if your content is sensitive, enabling a short stream delay (5-10 seconds) can give you a buffer to address issues before they reach your audience.

5. Manage Your Resources

RESOURCE MANAGEMENT is key to preventing your computer from being overwhelmed during a live stream.

- Close Unnecessary Applications: Streaming is resource-intensive. Close any unnecessary programs or browser tabs to free up your computer's processing power and reduce the risk of your stream crashing.

- Monitor CPU and Memory Usage: Keep an eye on your CPU and memory usage during the stream. If either is consistently high, consider lowering your stream quality or closing additional programs to prevent your system from overheating or freezing.

6. Prepare for Technical Difficulties

NO MATTER HOW WELL you prepare, technical difficulties can still arise. Have a plan in place to deal with them quickly.

- Have a Backup Plan: Create a backup plan for common issues. For example, if your internet connection drops, have a mobile hotspot ready to switch to. If your software crashes, know how to quickly reboot and resume your stream.

- Create a Technical Checklist: Before going live, go through a checklist to ensure everything is in order. This should include checking your internet connection, camera, microphone, streaming software, and any other equipment.

- Communicate with Your Audience: If technical issues do arise, communicate with your audience. Let them know what's happening and what you're doing to fix it. Transparency can help maintain viewer trust even in the face of problems.

7. Test Everything Before Going Live

ONE OF THE BEST WAYS to prevent technical glitches during your live stream is to conduct a thorough test run.

- Run a Private Test Stream: Set up a private or unlisted stream to test your entire setup. This allows you to check for potential issues without an audience and make necessary adjustments.

- Check for Latency: Latency can be an issue if you're interacting with your audience in real-time. Test the latency during your private stream and adjust settings to minimize delays.

- Simulate Real Conditions: Test your stream under the same conditions as your actual live stream. Use the same internet connection, equipment, and streaming software to ensure that your test results are accurate.

8. Consider a Dedicated Streaming Setup

IF YOU'RE SERIOUS ABOUT live streaming, investing in a **dedicated streaming setup can significantly reduce technical issues.**

- Use a Streaming PC: A dedicated streaming PC, separate from your main computer, can handle the resource-heavy task of streaming. This reduces the strain on your primary computer and improves overall stability.

- Invest in a Capture Card: If you're streaming from a console or using a high-quality camera, a capture card can provide a stable, high-quality feed to your streaming software.

- Upgrade Your Internet Plan: If your current internet plan struggles to handle live streaming, consider upgrading to a plan with higher upload speeds and more reliable service.

Conclusion

LIVE STREAMING IS AN incredible way to connect with your audience in real-time, but technical glitches can quickly derail even the best-planned streams. By preparing your equipment, optimizing your setup, and having a plan in place to address potential issues, you can minimize disruptions and deliver a seamless live streaming experience. Remember, the key to a successful live stream is preparation, so take the time to test, troubleshoot, and optimize every aspect of your setup before going live. With these hacks, you'll be well on your way to glitch-free streaming and a more professional online presence.

How Do Bands Keep the Spark Alive Night After Night on Tour?

When your favorite band hits the road for a tour, delivering a high-energy performance every night is essential. But have you ever wondered how bands keep the excitement alive when they have to play the same setlist every single night? Let's explore some of the strategies used by bands to overcome this challenge and deliver unforgettable live shows.

Setlist Variations

ONE OF THE MOST COMMON tactics employed by bands is varying their setlist slightly from night to night. While the core songs remain the same, bands often rotate a few tracks in and out to keep the show fresh for themselves and the audience. This element of surprise adds an air of excitement, making each performance unique.

Spontaneous Jam Sessions

ANOTHER WAY BANDS INJECT life into their shows is through improvised jam sessions. These moments allow the musicians to showcase their raw talent and create spontaneous musical magic on stage. Audiences love the unpredictability of these sessions and appreciate the exclusive experience of witnessing live creativity unfold.

Interactive Elements

ENGAGING WITH THE AUDIENCE can also elevate a live performance. Bands often interact with the crowd, encouraging sing-alongs, call-and-response chants, or even inviting fans on stage.

These interactive elements create a sense of community and connection, transforming the concert into a shared experience rather than just a performance.

Visual Enhancements

INCORPORATING VISUAL effects, lighting, and stage design can significantly enhance the live show experience. Bands use these elements to create immersive atmospheres that complement their music and captivate the audience visually. Stunning visuals can breathe new life into familiar songs and elevate the overall impact of the performance.

Guest Appearances

SURPRISE GUEST APPEARANCES are a surefire way to keep the audience on their toes. When bands bring out special guests to join them on stage, it adds an element of excitement and unpredictability to the show. Fans love the thrill of unexpected collaborations and witnessing unique musical pairings that may never happen again.

Themed Shows

SOME BANDS OPT FOR themed shows to shake things up and keep their performances engaging. Whether it's playing an entire album from start to finish, covering songs from a specific era, or incorporating theatrical elements, themed shows offer a fresh take on the standard concert format. These themed performances provide a novel experience for fans and keep the band inspired throughout the tour.

Audience Participation

FINALLY, ENCOURAGING audience participation can inject energy into a live show. Bands may invite fans to contribute vocals, play instruments, or participate in interactive games during the performance. By involving the audience in the show, bands create a sense of camaraderie and make each concert feel like a collaborative celebration.

In conclusion, while touring presents the challenge of performing the same setlist night after night, bands have a variety of strategies at their disposal to keep their live shows exciting and captivating. By incorporating setlist variations, spontaneous jam sessions, interactive elements, visual enhancements, guest appearances, themed shows, and audience participation, bands continue to deliver dynamic performances that leave audiences eager for more.

Whether you're a seasoned concert-goer or a first-time attendee, witnessing a band's ability to keep the spark alive night after night is an exhilarating experience that speaks to the magic of live music. So, the next time your favorite band comes to town, rest assured that they have a repertoire of tricks up their sleeves to ensure that every show is a unique and unforgettable experience.

How to Maintain Passion Amidst Music Industry Struggles

In the pursuit of a successful music career, aspiring musicians often find themselves trapped in the relentless daily grind, yearning for stardom while facing challenges that can lead them to contemplate giving up on their dreams. This journey is not for the faint-hearted, as the music industry is a vast and competitive arena where talent alone is not always enough to guarantee recognition and success. Let's delve into the reasons behind why many musicians reach a breaking point and consider abandoning their musical aspirations because of music industry struggles.

1. Seeking Stardom: A Double-Edged Sword

THE ALLURE OF FAME and stardom can be a powerful driving force for musicians. The desire to be recognized, celebrated, and adored by audiences around the world fuels the ambition of many artists. However, the relentless pursuit of stardom can also become a double-edged sword, leading to feelings of disillusionment and dissatisfaction when immediate success is not achieved. It's essential for musicians to remember that success in the music industry is a marathon, not a sprint, and that real fulfillment comes from the passion for creating music itself, not just the pursuit of fame.

2. Lack of Recognition: Unseen Efforts in a Crowded Industry

ONE OF THE MOST DISHEARTENING aspects that can cause musicians to reconsider their career choice is the lack of recognition for their talent and hard work. In an industry saturated with aspiring artists all striving for the spotlight, it's easy to feel invisible and overlooked. However, it's crucial for musicians to understand that recognition doesn't necessarily equate to success. Creating music for the sheer joy of expression and the love of the art itself can provide a deep sense of contentment and fulfillment that goes beyond external validation.

3. The Daily Grind: Persistence in the Face of Adversity

THE DAILY GRIND OF trying to make a mark in the music industry can be exhausting and demoralizing. Endless hours spent writing, composing, rehearsing, promoting, and performing can take a toll on even the most dedicated musicians. The pressure to constantly produce hit songs, gain followers, and secure record deals can lead to burnout and feelings of inadequacy. It's essential for musicians to find a balance between their artistic pursuits and their well-being, ensuring that they prioritize self-care and maintain a healthy perspective on their musical journey.

Lifting the Veil on the Music Industry

BEHIND THE GLITZ AND glamour of the music industry lies a challenging and competitive landscape that demands resilience, perseverance, and unwavering dedication from aspiring musicians. The road to success is paved with setbacks, rejections, and moments of self-doubt, but it's these very challenges that shape artists and propel them towards their goals. By embracing the process of creation, finding solace in artistic expression, and staying true to their passion for music, musicians can navigate the highs and lows of the industry with grace and resilience.

Remember, the journey to stardom is not a sprint but a marathon, and each step taken in the pursuit of one's musical dreams is a victory in itself. The path may be arduous, but the destination holds the promise of fulfillment beyond measure. So, let go of the need for instant gratification, embrace the creative process, and remember that true success lies in the boundless joy of making music that resonates with the soul.

In conclusion, the music industry is a challenging terrain, but it's also a wondrous realm where creativity knows no bounds and passion fuels the soul. Don't give up on your dreams at the first sign of adversity; instead, let your love for music be your guiding light through the darkest of days. Keep creating, keep believing, and one day, you might just find yourself basking in the radiance of stardom you've always dreamed of.

Let your music be your voice, your beacon, and your legacy – for in the end, it's not about the fame, but the profound impact your artistry can have on the world.

Stay strong, stay inspired, and keep making music that moves hearts and souls. The stage is yours – seize it with unwavering determination and unbridled passion. The world is waiting to be serenaded by your extraordinary talent.

Unleashing Your Inner Rockstar: A Guide

Are you feeling stuck in a musical rut? Does the mere thought of creating music evoke more feelings of frustration than inspiration? Don't worry; you're not alone. Many aspiring musicians go through phases where they contemplate giving up on their passion. But fear not, dear frustrated musician, for there are ways to reignite that creative fire within you and keep the music alive.

Embracing the Journey

Making music is an incredible journey filled with ups and downs, twists and turns. One common reason why people consider throwing in the towel is **boredom** . The repetitive nature of practicing, writing, and performing can sometimes lead to a sense of monotony. So, how can you combat this feeling and breathe new life into your musical endeavors?

The Battle Against Writer's Block

Writer's block is the arch-nemesis of every musician. Those moments when the melodies refuse to flow and the lyrics seem to evade your grasp can be incredibly disheartening. But remember, it's all part of the process. Take a step back, go for a walk, or engage in activities that have nothing to do with music. Sometimes, the best ideas come when you least expect them.

Seeking Inspiration

To reignite your passion for making music, you must actively seek inspiration. Listen to a wide variety of genres, attend live performances, or collaborate with other musicians. Embrace new sounds, techniques, and perspectives. The world is brimming with inspiration; all you have to do is open your ears and your mind to it.

Confidence is Key

Another reason why many musicians consider giving up is **lack of confidence** . It's easy to get bogged down by self-doubt, especially in an industry as competitive as the music world. Remember, every musician, no matter how successful, has faced moments of insecurity. Believe in your talent, work hard, and trust the process. Confidence is a muscle that grows stronger with each challenge you overcome.

Find Your Support System

Surround yourself with people who believe in you and your music. Whether it's friends, family, or fellow musicians, having a strong support system can make a world of difference. Share your struggles and triumphs with them, seek feedback, and celebrate your achievements together. Remember, you don't have to navigate this musical journey alone.

Conclusion

Making music is a beautiful, albeit challenging, pursuit. It's okay to feel frustrated or uninspired at times—it's all part of the process. Embrace the highs and the lows, seek inspiration from the world around you, and most importantly, believe in yourself. Your inner rockstar is ready to shine; all you have to do is unleash it.

Now, go forth, create, and let your music be the soundtrack to your journey.

Optimizing Band Practice: Effective Rehearsal Strategies

Band practice is essential for honing your group's sound, tightening performances, and building chemistry among members. But not all rehearsals are created equal. Without structure and strategy, band practice can quickly turn into unproductive jam sessions. To make the most out of your time together, it's important to adopt effective rehearsal strategies. Here are some tips to optimize your band practice and ensure every session brings you closer to your musical goals.

1. Set Clear Goals for Each Practice

ONE OF THE MOST IMPORTANT steps in optimizing band practice is setting clear, specific goals for each session. Having a shared objective keeps everyone focused and ensures that the practice time is productive.

- Song-Specific Goals: Decide which songs you want to work on and what you hope to achieve, whether it's nailing the transitions, tightening up the rhythm section, or perfecting vocal harmonies.

- Technical Goals: Focus on improving specific technical aspects, like timing, dynamics, or tuning. Set aside time for each member to address any technical challenges they're facing.

- Performance Goals: If you have a gig coming up, dedicate time to running through your setlist in order, working on stage presence, and practicing crowd interaction.

2. Create a Structured Practice Schedule

A WELL-STRUCTURED REHEARSAL plan helps keep the session on track and ensures that all necessary areas are covered.

- Warm-Up: Start with a warm-up session to get everyone in the right headspace. This could include running through scales, a quick jam, or playing a few easy songs to loosen up.

- Focus on New Material: Tackle new songs or parts of songs while everyone's fresh. Work on learning new sections, arranging, or experimenting with different sounds and styles.

- Review and Refine: Spend time refining the songs you're already familiar with. This is where you work on tightening up arrangements, fixing any issues, and ensuring everyone is on the same page.

- Full Run-Through: If you're preparing for a live performance, do a full run-through of your setlist, treating it like a real show. This helps you identify any weak spots and builds confidence.

- Debrief: End each session with a quick debrief. Discuss what went well, what needs more work, and set goals for the next practice.

3. Communicate Effectively

EFFECTIVE COMMUNICATION is key to a successful band practice. It ensures that everyone is heard, issues are addressed promptly, and the rehearsal runs smoothly.

- Respectful Feedback: Provide constructive feedback in a way that's respectful and supportive. Focus on what can be improved rather than just pointing out mistakes.

- Active Listening: Make sure everyone has a chance to voice their thoughts and concerns. Encourage active listening, where band members really pay attention to each other's ideas and input.

- Delegate Roles: Assign roles to ensure everything runs smoothly. For instance, one person can be responsible for timekeeping, another for setting up equipment, and another for managing the setlist.

4. Record Your Practices

RECORDING YOUR PRACTICES can be a game-changer. It allows you to objectively assess your performance and identify areas that need improvement.

- Audio Recording: Use a simple recording device or smartphone to capture your sessions. Listen back to identify timing issues, pitch problems, or areas where the arrangement feels off.

- Video Recording: Recording video can help with stage presence and performance dynamics. Watch the footage together and discuss what worked and what didn't.

- Review Together: Set aside time to review the recordings as a band. This can be done at the end of practice or before the next session. Discuss what you hear and make notes on what needs to be worked on.

5. Prioritize Individual Practice

WHILE BAND PRACTICE is crucial, individual practice is equally important. Each member should come to rehearsal prepared, knowing their parts inside and out.

- Practice at Home: Make sure everyone practices their parts on their own time. This ensures that band practice can be focused on playing together, rather than learning individual parts.

- Set Practice Expectations: Agree on what each member should work on between rehearsals. This could be learning new material, improving technique, or memorizing lyrics.

- Provide Resources: Share practice materials like chord charts, tabs, or recordings to help everyone prepare effectively.

6. Focus on Dynamics and Tightness

A TIGHT, WELL-REHEARSED band pays attention to dynamics and how each part fits into the whole. Working on these aspects can take your performance to the next level.

- Volume Control: Work on controlling your dynamics, ensuring that each instrument is balanced and no one is overpowering the mix. Practice playing sections softly, then gradually building up to louder parts.

- Timing: Use a metronome during practice to lock in your timing. Practice difficult sections slowly at first, then gradually increase the tempo.

- Break It Down: If a particular section is giving you trouble, break it down and practice it in isolation. Once everyone has it down, put it back into the context of the whole song.

7. Keep Things Fun and Fresh

WHILE STRUCTURE AND discipline are important, don't forget to keep the joy in your rehearsals. A positive, relaxed atmosphere can do wonders for creativity and group cohesion.

- Incorporate Jams: Set aside time for free-form jamming. This can be a great way to explore new ideas, develop chemistry, and keep things fun.

- Celebrate Progress: Acknowledge milestones and improvements, no matter how small. This helps maintain motivation and keeps the mood upbeat.

- Mix It Up: If you're feeling stuck, try changing up your routine. Play a cover song for fun, swap instruments, or experiment with new genres and styles.

Conclusion

OPTIMIZING BAND PRACTICE is about finding the right balance between structure, communication, and creativity. By setting clear goals, maintaining a structured schedule, and ensuring that everyone is prepared and engaged, you can make the most of your rehearsal time. Remember, the ultimate goal is to create great music together, so keep the atmosphere positive, stay open to new ideas, and always strive for improvement. With the right strategies in place, your band will not only sound better but also enjoy the journey of making music together.

Also by Neil J Milliner

Artful Investments: Enhancing Your Property Value Through Fine Art
E-commerce SEO Strategies: Selling Online Successfully
Fast Track Your Songwriting Career-Essential Tips and Hints to
Master Your Craft and Build a Lasting Career
The Ultimate Singer's Guide-Practical Tips to Improve Your Voice and
Achieve Your Vocal Dreams
Branding & Networking Success for Bands
Mastering Fan Engagement-Pro-Level Hints to Create Authentic
Connections and Build Loyalty
Mastering Live Performance & Touring-Pro Level Tips and Hints to
Elevate Your Stage Presence and Tour Like a Pro
Music Production Mastery-Step-by-Step Tutorials to Fast-Track Your
Way to Professional Success
The Musician's Tech Toolbox-Essential Technical Tips and Equipment
Know-How for Musicians
The Ultimate Musician's Website Guide-Step-by-Step Tutorials to
Engage Fans and Showcase Your Talent

www.ingramcontent.com/pod-product-compliance
Lightning Source LLC
Chambersburg PA
CBHW051853130726
47987CB00002B/805